Praise for *Leading* *in Education*

In *Leading Within Systems of Inequity in Education*, Mary Rice-Boothe presents key leadership competencies that matter for people of color who step into formal equity leadership roles. Based on interviews with over 30 practicing equity leaders, relevant education research, and lessons gleaned from historical figures, this book is a valuable resource for leaders of color who are committed to sustaining themselves in the fraught work of making education more equitable for all children and youth.

> —**Decoteau J. Irby**, associate professor of educational policy
> studies at the University of Illinois at Chicago and author of
> *Stuck Improving: Racial Equity and School Leadership*

Leading Within Systems of Inequity in Education is a must-read for all leaders aiming to heal themselves on their journey to liberate the education spaces they occupy. Mary Rice-Boothe leverages powerful accounts from ABILPOC equity leaders and her own lived experiences to provide a playbook and North Star for those who find themselves struggling to navigate these difficult spaces with self-awareness, certainty, love, and community.

> —**Carmita Semaan**, founder and CEO, Surge Institute

I cannot think of a recent book that has greater implications for equity-focused leaders than *Leading Within Systems of Inequity in Education: A Liberation Guide for Leaders of Color.* We have struggled in this nebulous space of equity-driven leadership for quite some time, without clear direction. Thank you for intersecting the "what" and the "how" of this critically important work. There is no question that *Leading Within Systems of Inequity in Education* provides the necessary blueprint for leading the great liberation.

> —**Harrison Peters**, CEO, Men of Color in
> Educational Leadership (MCEL)

Mary Rice-Boothe courageously elevates the intersections of her own identity to help us understand the weight and responsibility placed on the role of the equity officer—a role predominantly held by leaders of color within a racist system of schools.

> —**Nancy B. Gutierrez**, EdLD, president and CEO,
> The Leadership Academy

There are books out there that I consider good reads while there are other books out there that I consider must-reads. What Mary Rice-Boothe has written is a must-read for all school leadership practitioners and aspiring school leaders. So much that is written for school leaders is written generically. What a breath of fresh air when there is a book written by a leader of color specifically for leaders of color that speaks to the specific reality of being a leader of color—particularly when the leader of color is tasked with leading in spaces that are not necessarily of color. I'm excited about this book, and I endorse it with no hesitation or reservation.

—**Principal Baruti Kafele**, retired principal, author, consultant

This timely volume shines with the compelling voices and stories of educators of color leading our educational systems toward equity. Artfully situated in multiracial educational histories and contemporary challenges, *Leading Within Systems of Inequity in Education* offers critical advice and insights for those working to dismantle racist systems and advance justice for the children in our schools.

—**Ann M. Ishimaru**, associate professor, University of Washington, and author of *Just Schools: Building Equitable Collaborations with Families & Communities*

In this powerful book, Mary Rice-Boothe reminds us that we can make substantive change within the system. Equity leaders will find Rice-Boothe's examples, reflective exercises, and frameworks useful, practical, and illuminating. This book is a must-read and a very valuable resource to those working for equity and racial justice within the system.

—**Terrance L. Green**, host of the Racially Just Schools podcast and associate professor of educational leadership and policy at the University of Texas at Austin

The hiring of any ABILPOC leader to advance issues of inequity is an important action. This book breaks the dissolution that one person, alone, can be all things in creating transformation within racist educational institutions. Mary Rice-Boothe has captured real lived experiences of equity officers and uses them as text to examine high-leverage competencies that every individual and district should be using as a mirror to examine their own equity efforts.

—**Ruby Ababio-Fernandez**, EdD, executive vice president, programming and development, Courageous Conversation

LEADING WITHIN SYSTEMS OF INEQUITY IN EDUCATION

MARY
RICE-BOOTHE

LEADING WITHIN SYSTEMS OF INEQUITY IN EDUCATION

A Liberation Guide for Leaders of Color

Arlington, Virginia USA

2800 Shirlington Road, Suite 1001 • Arlington, VA 22206 USA
Phone: 800-933-2723 or 703-578-9600 • Fax: 703-575-5400
Website: www.ascd.org • Email: member@ascd.org
Author guidelines: www.ascd.org/write

Penny Reinart, *Deputy Executive Director;* Genny Ostertag, *Managing Director, Book Acquisitions & Editing;* Susan Hills, *Senior Acquisitions Editor;* Mary Beth Nielsen, *Director, Book Editing;* Liz Wegner, *Editor;* Thomas Lytle, *Creative Director;* Donald Ely, *Art Director;* MaameYaa Danso/The Hatcher Group, *Graphic Designer;* Circle Graphics, *Typesetter;* Kelly Marshall, *Production Manager;* Shajuan Martin, *E-Publishing Specialist*

All web links in this book are correct as of the publication date below but may have become inactive or otherwise modified since that time. If you notice a deactivated or changed link, please email books@ascd.org with the words "Link Update" in the subject line. In your message, please specify the web link, the book title, and the page number on which the link appears.

PAPERBACK ISBN: 978-1-4166-3183-5   ASCD product #123014   n4/23
PDF EBOOK ISBN: 978-1-4166-3184-2; see Books in Print for other formats.
Quantity discounts are available: email programteam@ascd.org or call 800-933-2723, ext. 5773, or 703-575-5773. For desk copies, go to www.ascd.org/deskcopy.

Library of Congress Cataloging-in-Publication Data

Names: Rice-Boothe, Mary, author.
Title: Leading within systems of inequity in education : a liberation guide for leaders of color / Mary Rice-Boothe.
Description: Arlington, VA : ASCD, [2023] | Includes bibliographical references and index.
Identifiers: LCCN 2022051384 (print) | LCCN 2022051385 (ebook) | ISBN 9781416631835 (paperback) | ISBN 9781416631842 (pdf)
Subjects: LCSH: Minority school administrators—United States. | School management and organization—United States—Vocational guidance. | Racial justice in education—United States. | Educational leadership—United States. | Educational equalization—United States.
Classification: LCC LB2831.82 .R54 2023 (print) | LCC LB2831.82 (ebook) | DDC 371.2/0110973—dc23/eng/20230111
LC record available at https://lccn.loc.gov/2022051384
LC ebook record available at https://lccn.loc.gov/2022051385

32 31 30 29 28 27 26 25 24 23   1 2 3 4 5 6 7 8 9 10 11 12

For Dad. Thank you for laying the foundation. Miss you every day.

LEADING WITHIN SYSTEMS OF INEQUITY IN EDUCATION

A Liberation Guide for Leaders of Color

Introduction

So it is better to speak
remembering
we were never meant to survive.

—Audre Lorde, "A Litany for Survival"

I wrote this book for me and those like me. For me when I became a principal. For me when I became a nonprofit leader. For me when I became an equity officer.

Becoming an equity officer marked the first time I had a position without a job description, book, or standards and with the goal of building an equitable organization. I had the opportunity (and the accompanying angst) to create my own path. This was also the first role in my leadership journey in which all my intersectional identities were central to my work. I had always grappled with being a Black female leader within white spaces, but it wasn't my job to transparently share my ongoing journey toward racial consciousness and to leverage my experiences to support the development of others.

I always say that being a principal was the hardest job I ever had, but the past few years have been the most pivotal in my own consciousness. The combination of daily, deliberate unpacking of my biases, naming where white-dominant culture is showing up, dismantling inequities, and building new ones—all while managing my own double-consciousness—has awakened me to be a new type of leader: one who is grounded in my values and makes decisions through that lens.

I am thankful to have had a mentor from the first day of my leadership journey to the present. Whenever I am approaching a crossroads in my career, I reach out to him. What I most appreciate about our conversations is that he never gives me the answer. He just asks me the most difficult questions possible for me to grapple with. Trying to answer each question out loud is a brutal process, but I am so grateful when I make it to the other side every single time. Our last conversation came at the conclusion of three pivotal events for me:

- During a coaching call, I recognized that the only barrier between the leader I am versus the leader I want to be is *myself*, that I was operating deeply within a "right to comfort."
- In a conversation with a principal, he shared his feelings of dissonance in leading within a racialized institution; that staying aligned to values in every moment and every decision, and not compromising, can just be too much to bear.
- There has been a wave of anti–critical race theory laws across multiple states, including my home state of Texas.

In reading the transcripts of the interviews I conducted for this book with 35 practitioners and hearing them talk about the value of love and vulnerability, I must reflect on how much I lean into these values as well. Academically, I see their worth and impact, but I know that liberation is not an academic skill. I must wholeheartedly embrace these values and lead through them. Doing so places me as an outlier in some spaces. I need to be OK with that. I need to be able to embrace the dissonance, the double-consciousness that W. E. B. Du Bois (1897) identified so many decades ago—the notion that minoritized groups may view themselves through the eyes of their oppressors. This feeling has not gone away. As I stand in the towers of whiteness, I cannot avoid it.

I believe in liberation for minoritized people. I believe we need to teach true history. I believe being uncomfortable is part of the journey. I need to remain steadfast while not losing myself along the way.

Research Question and Methodology

Principals and superintendents have been in the K–12 space since its beginning, but the equity officer is a new position, with unique challenges. Over the course of a year, I had the opportunity to talk to 32 individuals who are in diversity, equity, and inclusion roles. I wanted to zone in on a position that is held overwhelmingly by people of color and that requires a wide-ranging skill set if the person is to be successful. I also spoke to 3 principals to provide a broader picture of leaders of color in a variety of leadership positions.

My initial research question that led me to writing this book was "How can an ABILPOC (Asian, Black, Indigenous, Latine, and people of color) leader be successful in a school system not designed for them when they were students and definitely not designed for them to lead?" However, I knew this question had been skillfully addressed in some spaces, although inequitable school systems still exist. So my essential question became this: "What skills does it take for an ABILPOC leader to dismantle systems of inequity and rebuild new ones where all students and adults can thrive?"

With that question in mind, I knew I could not—I *would* not—be an objective researcher collecting data. I leaned on the characteristics of portraiture to approach my research and writing. Sarah

Lawrence-Lightfoot (2016) defines her innovative methodology by saying, "We want to document what's strong and worthy, in great detail so that we might figure out ways of transporting those 'goods,' that goodness, to other settings and transforming them as well. That begins to describe some of the central tenets of portraiture" (p. 20).

Portraiture follows the rules of good research, but it is also about breaking the rules of traditional research. My primary method for data collection was video interviews. It was important for me to connect with each individual and hear them tell their story. Portraiture leans on "creating relationships with the people who you are interviewing and whose lives you're trying to capture, that are trusting and communicative and respectful; you are working on creating and sustaining authentic encounters" (Lawrence-Lightfoot, 2016, p. 22). Although I was not able to meet any of the interviewees in person, the video was important to see each person individually and create the context of each individual story. Sometimes the physical and facial reactions to a question told as much of a story as the words coming from the person's mouth. I came into each interview conscious of my own cultural identity and how it might affect my conversations with each person, be it a cross-race or a same-race conversation.

In my conversations with each leader, I asked the following questions:

For principals
1. Tell me your name, title, and what you do. How long have you been there?
2. What have you learned and unlearned about your identity, upbringing, and other formative experiences since taking on this role?
3. What challenges do you face as an [intersectional identity] system-level leader in a space dominated by whiteness?
4. What has challenged you as a leader of color leading through COVID, the racial reckoning, and current pushback?
5. How do you manage pushback from colleagues, supervisors, and/or the community?

6. What steps have you taken to dismantle systemic inequities and build new ones? What would you point to as quick wins?
7. What do you need from the larger education ecosystem to maintain and sustain you in your current role?
8. How do you practice self-care?

For equity officers
1. Tell me your name, title, and what you do. How long have you been there?
2. How are you positioned within your organization? Who do you report to?
3. What type of learning did you do and continue to do to feel confident to take on your role?
4. What have you learned and unlearned about your identity, upbringing, and other formative experiences since taking on this role?
5. What challenges do you face as an [intersectional identity] system-level leader in a space dominated by whiteness?
6. How do you manage pushback from colleagues? From those "above" you?
7. How do you know when to speak up when you see an inequity taking place or hear someone say something in a group meeting space? How do you usually approach this scenario?
8. How have you created an informal or formal team of colleagues who are championing this work with you?
9. What do you need from the education system to set you up for success?
10. How do you practice self-care?
11. What advice would you give to someone about to start a diversity/equity officer role?

See Figure I.1 for general demographic information about the persons interviewed. Figure I.2 provides additional details about these individuals and the school systems they serve.

FIGURE I.1

High-Level Overview of Leaders Interviewed

Role	Type of Organization	Gender	Race/Ethnicity
Equity Officer (32)	5 charters 26 districts 1 nonprofit	20 women 12 men	2 Asian 24 Black 3 Latine 3 More than one race/ethnicity
Principal (3)	1 charter 2 districts	2 women 1 man	2 Black 1 Latine

FIGURE I.2

Information on Each Leader Interviewed

Name	Role	Size/Type School System Small: Fewer than 50,000 students Medium: 50,000–100,000 students Large: More than 100,000 students	State	Gender	Race/Ethnicity*
Aaron	Equity Officer	Small, district	MA	M	Black
Angela	Equity Officer	Medium, district	TX	F	Black
Benny	Equity Officer	Large, charter	NY	M	Latino
Chalisa	Equity Officer	Small, district	TX	F	Black
Danielle	Equity Officer	Large, district	FL	F	Black
Denise**	Equity Officer	Medium, charter	PA	F	Black
David	Equity Officer	Large, district	MD	M	Black
Gilmara	Equity Officer	Medium, district	IA	F	Latina
Henry**	Equity Officer	Large, district	MA	M	Black
Jeremy**	Equity Officer	Medium, district	CO	M	Latino
Jessica	Equity Officer	Small, district	MA	F	Black
Johnny	Equity Officer	Small, district	MA	M	Asian
Kori	Equity Officer	Medium, charter	DC	F	Black
Laurice	Equity Officer	Small, district	WI	F	More than one ethnicity/race
Lisa	Equity Officer	Large, district	VA	F	Black
Marco	Principal	Small, charter	CA	M	Latino
Mariane	Equity Officer	Medium, district	CA	F	More than one ethnicity/race

Name	Role	Size/Type School System Small: Fewer than 50,000 students Medium: 50,000–100,000 students Large: More than 100,000 students	State	Gender	Race/Ethnicity*
Maurice	Equity Officer	Large, district	IL	M	Black
Mekka	Equity Officer	Large, charter	MA	F	Black
Michael	Equity Officer	Large, district	TN	M	Black
Monica	Equity Officer	Large, district	FL	F	More than one ethnicity/race
Nancy**	Equity Officer	Medium, district	TX	F	Black
Nasif	Equity Officer	Small, district	WI	M	Black
Nicole	Equity Officer	Large, district	NY	F	Black
Owen**	Equity Officer	Large, charter	NY	M	Black
Patricia**	Equity Officer	Small, district	CA	F	Black
Patty**	Equity Officer	Medium, district	CA	F	Black
Shakira	Equity Officer	Small, district	CA	F	Black
Shari	Equity Officer	Small, district	WI	F	Black
Shirley**	Principal	Medium, district	TX	F	Black
Stephanie	Equity Officer	Medium, district	TX	F	Black
Stephen	Equity Officer	Nonprofit	CA	M	Asian
TaraShaun	Principal	Large, district	IL	F	Black
Tauheedah	Equity Officer	Large, district	GA	F	Black
Tommy	Equity Officer	Large, district	GA	M	Black

* Self-identified
** Name changed

Vocabulary

The following are terms that I will be using throughout this book. I want to define them before we dive in any further:

- **ABILPOC**—Asian, Black, Indigenous, Latine, people of color.
- **Internalized oppression**—When oppressed people accept, believe, and act on the negative image placed upon them from their oppressor (Hegde, 2022).

- **Intersectionality**—The study of how overlapping or intersecting social identities, particularly minority identities, relate to systems and structures of oppression, domination, or discrimination (Crenshaw, 1989).
- **Liberation**—The creation of relationships, societies, communities, organizations, and collective spaces characterized by equity, fairness, and the implementation of systems for the allocation of goods, services, benefits, and rewards that support the full participation of each human and the promotion of their full humanness (Love et al., 2008).
- **Minoritized**—The term *minoritized* changes the noun *minority* to a verb to emphasize how institutional actions have labeled certain populations, leading to them having a different experience from those with power (Leadership Academy, 2021).
- **People of color**—Historically disenfranchised Americans, Black/ African, Hispanic/Latine, Asian/Pacific Islanders, Native-Indigenous Indians, and biracial people.
- **Systemic racism**—The legalization of white domination infused in all aspects of society including history, culture, politics, economics, education, and other structural institutions. This form of racism routinely gives an advantage to white people while producing adverse outcomes for people of color (Racial Equity Tools, 2020).
- **White-dominant culture**—The dominant, unquestioned standards of thinking, behaving, deciding, and knowing. These standards come from a white, Western tradition—while devaluing cultural practices from other parts of the world (Racial Equity Tools, 2020).
- **Whiteness**—Whiteness is not about skin color alone. It operates at all times and on all levels. Whiteness shows up in practice, perspectives, and experiences purported to be commonly shared by all but are, in reality, only consistently afforded to white people (Racial Equity Tools, 2020).

Chapter Topics and Format

Chapter 1 explores how students of color have experienced school in the United States, the role of ABILPOC leaders in history, and how they currently see themselves in the school system. Chapter 2 introduces a set of competencies that leaders can use to be successful within white spaces and to dismantle those spaces and create a new system.

The remaining chapters break down the competencies and what they look like in action. Chapter 3 gives leaders reflective exercises they can engage in as they unpack their role in upholding systemic racism in the schools and systems where they work. The chapter also discusses how leaders can operate outside their comfort zone, knowing that it is one way of decentering white-dominant culture and whiteness. In Chapter 4, leaders are provided methods for practicing self-care individually and collectively as they continue working to dismantle the systemic racism they face daily. Chapter 5 gives leaders language for how to name what they see even amid worry about being labeled as "difficult" or "angry." Chapter 6 discusses ways leaders can attend to relationships and embrace coconspirators across race, culture, and perspectives. Readers will also learn how to create a coalition of liberatory leaders by building the capacity of others. Chapter 7 inspires leaders to be patient but persistent in dismantling white spaces, knowing it will take time to create new liberatory education systems. It encourages them to take a stand in pursuit of a liberatory education system even if the concept is unpopular. It also suggests ways for ABILPOC leaders to act to change everyday systemic racism in terms of policies, procedures, and systems.

The final chapter explains how ABILPOC leaders can leverage coconspirators such as board members, superintendents, and members of influential community organizations, all of whom are responsible for creating a working environment that provides opportunity for everyone to thrive. It provides concrete examples of what a system designed for the ABILPOC leader would look like and the steps needed to get there.

Chapters 3 through 8 begin with a story from a current or former ABILPOC system-level leader who shares leadership experiences. These chapters end with a bulleted list of main ideas from the chapter; a list of questions to guide individual, partner, team, or community reflection or further exploration to extend the learning beyond the text; and a list of resources to support the continuing effort to lean into and learn about the competencies shared in the chapter.

Audience

Writing a book focused on so many races and ethnicities runs the risk of painting all Asians, Black people, Indigenous peoples, Latine, and people of color as having one story. As members of minoritized communities, we have never been, nor will we ever be, a monolith. Even within these categories such as "Asian" and "Latine," there are so many different countries, cultures, and experiences represented that putting them into one category can and has been problematic. Our histories and experiences within the United States are different. However, as oppressed communities, we have turned to each other for examples, support, and solidarity. This book highlights a small number of communities' experiences with the public school system in the United States. There are many stories and communities missing, but it's the interconnectedness of cultures that this book seeks to highlight.

If you are a leader of color whose North Star is creating an equitable school system, this book is specifically for you. If you have been minoritized by the education system, this book is for you. If you are leading within an education system that is not reaching its goal of serving its minoritized students and you want to understand the skills you need to break down the white spaces, this book is for you.

Author's Note

Thank you to Audre Lorde. Her words, her guidance, her influence are all over this book. She holds hands with bell hooks. Together they are the foundation of this work. Their experiences, encouragement, and push toward liberation motivate me. Audre Lorde said we don't live single-issue lives. We also don't live in isolation. Yes, Black folx made me. I'm African American; I'm an able-bodied, cisgender, heterosexual woman. So that's my story, my lens, my perspective; but I can't be liberated and seek liberation for only those who share my intersectional identities. So *Leading Within Systems of Inequity in Education: A Liberation Guide for Leaders of Color* is for my people. To my culture and to all other cultures that have been systemically marginalized in the United States, I offer these words of love to provide a space for reflection and a sense that you are not alone. There are many others fighting within their school systems with you. No one has achieved liberation, yet we are trying every day.

I do not claim to speak for every Asian, Black, Indigenous, Latine, and person of color working in leadership in a school system. It will never be my goal. It's not possible. The goal in writing this book, in sharing the stories, in giving this advice, is liberation. Disagree with what I propose. I get it! Take parts of it. Great! Take it all in. Fantastic! Do what works for you. I am here to cheer you on from the sideline.

1

How Did We Get Here?

I have been in the world, but not of it.

—W. E. B. Du Bois

Leaders who are Asian, Black, Indigenous, Latine, and people of color (ABILPOC) matter. When students see educators who look like them, they excel, as measured by increases in attendance, academic achievement, and high school completion and fewer instances of discipline (Bartanen & Grissom, 2019). But the longevity of ABILPOC leaders is shrinking. Every day I get emails alerting me to a new job posting for a superintendent, a principal, or an equity officer. School systems are looking for someone to help them fix a problem—namely, a 400-year-old problem of changing a system designed to oppress and minoritize the students walking through the doors of many public schools every day.

Today in the United States, roughly 53 percent of public school students are young people of color. Breaking that down further, Latine students accounted for 28 percent of public school students in the fall of 2020 (NCES, 2022b). Schools are growing more racially diverse every year, but the percentages of ABILPOC district leaders are not growing at the same rate.

Even though the school system in the United States was not created for Asians, Black people, Indigenous people, Latine, and people of color, history shows that we continually and consistently come together to support our families and community despite the most difficult conditions. ABILPOC leaders have used the experiences, wisdom, and insights of their ancestors and brought them to work every day to dismantle systems of oppression and create a new, equitable system. It's now time to bring those efforts, skills, and dispositions to the forefront so that other new and experienced ABILPOC leaders can join the movement to create a just and equitable system for everyone.

Hidden Provocateurs

In March 1865, the U.S. Congress passed an act to create the federal Bureau of Refugees, Freedmen, and Abandoned Lands, commonly known as the Freedmen's Bureau, to help millions of former Black slaves and poor white people in the South in the aftermath of the Civil War. The Freedmen's Bureau provided food, housing, and medical aid; established schools; and offered legal assistance (Spraggins, 1970). During its existence, the Freedmen's Bureau created a total of 4,000 schools educating more than 150,000 pupils. However, the bureau was prevented from fully carrying out its programs due to a shortage of funds and personnel, along with the politics of race and Reconstruction. In the summer of 1872, Congress, responding in part to pressure from white Southerners and President Ulysses S. Grant, dismantled the Freedmen's Bureau (Spraggins, 1970).

The Haines Normal and Industrial Institute

In 1883, after the work of the Freedmen's Bureau, Lucy Laney founded a school for Black children in Augusta, Georgia. A child of slaves, Laney learned to read during a time when teaching a slave to read was illegal. She defied societal norms and worked as a teacher in Macon, Milledgeville, and Savannah, Georgia, for 10 years before deciding to open a school of her own (Feger, 1942).

The school was intended to be for girls only, but a few neighborhood boys arrived, and she accepted them. By its second year, the school had an enrollment of 250 students. Laney needed more support. Her initial request was turned down, but philanthropist Francine E. H. Haines later donated $10,000 for the school. Laney changed the school's name to the Haines Normal and Industrial Institute in honor of her benefactor and to indicate the school's mission to support industrial and teacher training. In her 50 years as principal, Laney served students and prepared teachers for their role (Feger, 1942).

The Peabody Indian School and the Carlisle Indian School

Two years after Laney opened her school in Georgia, the Peabody Indian School in Nevada was opened by Sarah Winnemucca, a self-educated Northern Paiute Indian. Winnemucca wanted to create a school taught by and for Indigenous peoples. In her first year, she taught 26 Paiute children, many of whom spoke no English. As soon as the children could speak and understand some English, she began teaching them to read and write the language (Peabody, 1886).

The Peabody Indian School was opened amid an era of assimilationist policies. On March 3, 1819, the U.S. Congress had enacted the Civilization Fund Act, authorizing the president, "in every case where he shall judge improvement in the habits and condition of such Indians practicable," to "employ capable persons of good moral character" to introduce to any tribe adjoining a frontier settlement the "arts of civilization" (Gere, 2005).

This act led the way for Indigenous children to be forcibly separated from their families on the reservation and be placed in schools that enacted assimilationist practices. By the 1880s, there were 60 schools for 6,200 Indigenous students, including day schools and boarding schools. The schools' enrollment was at its peak in the 1970s, with more than 60,000 attending. Schools remained open until passage of the

1978 Indian Child Welfare Act, which granted Indigenous parents the right to deny placement of their children in these schools (Gere, 2005).

Unlike the Peabody Indian School, the Carlisle Indian School in Carlisle, Pennsylvania, opened by Colonel Richard Henry Pratt, lived out the motto "Kill the Indian, Save the Man." At Carlisle, when new students arrived, school staff guessed how old they were, set their "birthday," and gave them an age. Then the students were assigned a Christian name. Students' hair was cut, despite the fact that, for many tribes, the only time a person's hair was cut was when someone died. Their traditional clothing was exchanged for uniforms and hard-toed shoes, and they were banned from speaking their languages. Boys were trained to become laborers and girls to become domestic workers. These children were cut off from their families and often experienced physical and sexual abuse (Zitkala-Sa, 2000).

At the Peabody School, the goal was to help children to be proud of their traditions and history. There was a focus on caring for one another and respecting the land. Sarah Winnemucca always reminded them of their Paiute history and heritage. Her objective was to make her students teachers, to use the older ones as assistants and substitutes, and to encourage the students to undertake their own self-education, as she had done (Peabody, 1887).

Winnemucca received attention for the success of her school from journalists and other educators; however, her hopes of receiving funds from the U.S. government never materialized. A Washington official arrived at the school in the summer of 1886. He told Winnemucca that the school could not receive any aid from the Reserved Fund for Indian Education unless she surrendered leadership of the school. She refused. She continued to teach for three more years, with remarkable success. She closed the school in 1888 (Zitkala-Sa, 2000).

The Aoy School

In 1848, at the end of the Mexican-American War, the Treaty of Guadalupe Hidalgo established that Mexicans in the newly acquired territories of the United States would be racially classified as white. However, the de facto exclusion of Mexican Americans from designated white spaces, particularly schools, was widespread, and especially common in Texas (González, 2000). The state of Texas established a permanent system of common public schools in 1854 with the Common School Law. The law was quickly amended to stipulate that "no school shall be entitled to funding in connection to this act unless the English language is principally taught." The amended law, targeted at both German immigrants and former Mexican citizens, attempted to impose English as the only language in public schools (Gutfreund, 2019).

Unlike the strict, race-based, de jure segregated schooling for African Americans in the South and the forced enrollment into boarding schools for Indigenous peoples, the practice of segregating Mexican American pupils was oftentimes conducted outside the legal structure (Gutfreund, 2019). Mexican American children in the Southwest and in states including Iowa, Oklahoma, and Kansas were placed in "Mexican classrooms" or schools beginning in the early 1900s. White administrators defended this practice, saying that it was a result of English language deficiencies, although many "Mexican" students spoke only English. The "Mexican schools" were taught primarily by white teachers who punished students if they spoke Spanish. Furthermore, white parents objected to their children being schooled with what they called "dirty and diseased" Mexicans (San Miguel, 1987).

Two years after Sarah Winnemucca opened the Peabody School, Mexican parents founded the Aoy Preparatory School in El Paso, Texas, in protest against the common school law, and hired teacher Olives Villanueva Aoy (San Miguel, 1987). Originally from Spain, Aoy had spent time in Mexico, and he converted to become a Mormon before traveling to Texas. In 1888, the school board in El Paso incorporated Aoy's school on a segregated basis, and it eventually became known as the Mexican Preparatory School. A vacant customhouse building was made available to Aoy in 1891, and with two assistants, he taught English to nearly one hundred 1st and 2nd grade students. He also supplied them with food and clothing and cared for their health. By 1897, the small school had grown to an enrollment of 200 students with a staff of three teachers. In 1899, the school board built a six-room schoolhouse, named Aoy School, that could accommodate

300 students. In 1900, the Aoy School was holding double sessions and reported an enrollment of 500—the largest enrollment of any El Paso school at that time (San Miguel, 1987).

The bilingual nature of the school shifted over time, and by 1905, students were sent to the school by directive: "All Spanish-speaking pupils in the city who live west of Austin Street will report at the Aoy School, corner of 7th and Campbell, English-speaking Mexican children will attend the school of the district in which they live" (San Miguel, 1987, p. 165). "Mexican schools" such as this one, originally created to preserve the Spanish language and Mexican culture, were used as a means of cultural, linguistic, and social subordination in the white-dominant society (Zambrana & Hurtado, 2015).

Japanese Language Schools and Developments During World War II

The Gold Rush of the late 1840s and 1850s brought a large Chinese population to California. As Chinese immigration slowed, Japanese immigration increased, with new arrivals settling primarily in California and Hawaii. Japanese immigration also brought Japanese language schools. The schools were created to complement the traditional public schools by providing classes to children to maintain or gain the ability to learn their native language. However, these schools prompted suspicion from American politicians who wanted schools only to assimilate new immigrants (Gutfreund, 2019).

Then came the bombing of Pearl Harbor. On February 19, 1942, President Franklin D. Roosevelt issued Executive Order 9066. It authorized the army to "designate military areas" from which "any persons may be excluded." The War Relocation Authority (WRA) was created and developed 10 "Relocation Centers" that held 110,000 Japanese Americans.

The WRA's first head of education, Lucy W. Adams, was the superintendent of schools on the Navajo reservation in Arizona under the "Indian New Deal," through which the administration had been experimenting with progressive methods of education under federal authority for almost a decade. Under Adams's leadership, a group of education students from Stanford developed a handbook for how the schools in the 10 camps would look. They viewed the camps as an opportunity to achieve the progressive vision of integrating schooling with the productive life of work and experience.

Americanization classes were central to camp schooling. The classes focused on indoctrinating the younger generation of Japanese Americans with "American values" that would ensure their loyalty and best prepare them for an assimilated life after the war. A ritual in relocation camp schools was the salute to the flag, followed by singing of the song "America (My Country, 'Tis of Thee)."

In response to unrest in the relocation camps in the fall of 1942, the WRA instituted a questionnaire to separate the "loyal" from the "disloyal." Two questions were the most important (Lyon, n.d.): (1) "If the opportunity presents itself and you are found qualified, would you be willing to volunteer for the Army Nurse Corps or the WAAC [Women's Army Auxiliary Corps]?" and (2) "Will you swear unqualified allegiance to the United States of America and forswear any form of allegiance or obedience to the Japanese emperor, or any other foreign government, power, or organization?"

Based on answers to the two questions, the "loyal" were deemed eligible to enlist in the army or to leave the concentration camps to "resettle" in areas away from the West Coast, whereas the "disloyal" or "no-nos" (those who answered no to both questions) were sent to the Tule Lake, California, relocation camp (Lyon, n.d.).

This transition also shut down WRA-operated schools. As a replacement, members of the camps opened their own Japanese language schools, operated under the Japanese Language School Board. At the same time, eight underground "school republics" emerged, operating as self-contained systems against WRA regulations and unrelated to the Japanese Language School Board (James, 1987). These schools and private tutors relegated many of the older Japanese cultural practices to a secondary role and instead tried to emulate the current curriculum and military exercises of modern Japan. The explicit purpose of many of these schools and tutors was to prepare students for immediate "return" to Japan. Many parents had no intention of returning but still leveraged their children's enrollment into these schools as a symbolic protest within the politics of camp life (James, 1987).

The "Problem" Populations and Intercultural Cooperation

Throughout the history of the United States, minoritized groups have been labeled a "problem," and schools have been used as a weapon to push assimilation. As the changing demographics of students and waves of immigration have continued, the playbook for assimilation and oppression has been repeated again and again.

At the same time, individual and collective members of each community have created counter-educational experiences to maintain language, history, and cultural traditions. Although these stories show how communities fought singularly, their cross-community collaboration was also evident. In a speech in Boston in 1869, Frederick Douglass argued against the Chinese Exclusion Act, stating that the Chinese should be allowed to immigrate and become citizens. He presented his vision of a composite nation under conditions of "perfect human equality" (Araiza, 2013).

The Plan of San Diego was drafted in San Diego, Texas, in 1915 by a group of Mexican and Tejano rebels who hoped to secure the secession of Arizona, New Mexico, California, and Texas from the United States and return them to the Indigenous nations. Their goal was to create a racial utopia for Indigenous peoples, Mexican Americans, Asian Americans, and African Americans (Johnson, 2005).

In Los Angeles in the summer of 1943, sailors, soldiers, and Marines wearing zoot suits led a 10-day violent rampage against young Mexican men. The "Zoot Suit Riots" resulted in the local NAACP banding together with the Mexican American Community Service Organization to demand accountability from the U.S. Navy (Araiza, 2013).

The Third World Liberation Front (TWLF), formed in the late 1960s, was composed of multiethnic coalitions of student organizations at San Francisco State College (now San Francisco State University) and the University of California at Berkeley. The TWLF went on strike to fight for relevant, accessible education for and by ABILPOC students. Asian American, Black, Chicana/o, and Indigenous students joined together, leading to the creation of the first Black Studies Department and School of Ethnic Studies in the United States (Araiza, 2013).

Intercultural collaboration of minoritized communities has occurred throughout U.S. history. It continues today.

Today's Provocateurs

The voices and forces of minoritized communities have led to laws intended to further propel an integrated public school system. In Mendez v. Westminster School District (1946), the plaintiffs demanded an end to the segregation of more than 5,000 Mexican and Mexican American students in the various school districts in Orange County, California. Judge Paul J. McCormick's finding stated that the students' rights to equal schooling should be protected under the Equal Protection clause of the Fourteenth Amendment (González, 2000). The Brown v. Board of Education decision (1954) also leveraged the Fourteenth Amendment to say separate schooling was not equal for Black students in the United States (Fairclough, 2000). The 1978 Indian Child Welfare Act acknowledged that Indigenous children were being removed from their homes and communities at a much higher rate than non-Indigenous children. The act established standards for the placement of Indigenous children in foster and adoptive homes and enabled tribes and families to be involved in child welfare cases (Gere, 2005).

Although these acts led to the integration of classrooms, schools, and school systems across the United States, they also led to an exodus of Asian, Black, Indigenous and Latine leaders. Today in the United States, people of color make up 21 percent of teachers (Taie & Goldring, 2020), 22 percent of principals, and 8.6 percent of superintendents (NCES, 2022a). Principals, superintendents, and equity officers each play significant roles in a school system, but as a leader who has been minoritized myself, I understand firsthand that our experiences and challenges are unique and require attention and support.

The Principal

In May 1954, there were almost 82,000 Black educators in segregated schools, and their presence in schools and classrooms significantly affected and improved the learning experiences for their students (Karpinski, 2006). Many Black educators played a variety of roles inside and outside the classroom to provide a learning environment that supported the needs of Black students. Curriculum developed for Black schools celebrated Black contributions and culture and raised racial consciousness (Fairclough, 2000).

The 1954 Brown v. Board of Education decision led to limited opportunities for Black educators in the newly integrated schools. Black principals and teachers left their positions in large numbers because of demotion within white school systems or not being offered a position at all. The number of Black teachers was also reduced. Although thousands of Black students were transferred to white schools, white students were rarely transferred to Black schools because of the inadequacy of the facilities and racism (Fairclough, 2000).

We now have a different landscape when it comes to ABILPOC school leaders. According to the U.S. Department of Education, in 2017–18, about 78 percent of public school principals were white, 11 percent were Black, and 9 percent were Hispanic. Those who were Asian, American Indian/Alaska Native, or of two or more races each made up 1 percent of public school principals, and those who were Pacific Islander made up less than 1 percent (NCES, 2022a).

The percentage of public school principals who were white was lower in 2017–18 than in 1999–2000: 78 percent versus 82 percent. In contrast, the percentage who were Hispanic was higher in 2017–18 than in 1999–2000: 9 percent versus 5 percent. The percentages of Black principals were not measurably different across these two school years (NCES, 2022a). The current number of school leaders of color is not equivalent to the students of color coming through public school doors every day.

Black principals often work in underresourced schools that have large minority student populations. Latine principals usually come into the position after being typecast into administrative positions of symbolic or practical significance to the minoritized community, such as director of bilingual education programs (Valverde & Brown, 1988).

The Superintendent

A school superintendent leads a school system, which comes in several shapes and sizes. Despite the differences, the position itself involves the same responsibilities. As defined by Hodgkinson and Montenegro (1999), "Superintendents are charged with the responsibility of ensuring an effective teaching and learning process, as well as with the oversight of the financial, legal, and personnel operations aspects of the system" (p. 7). The route to the superintendency almost always involves being a teacher, then a principal, then a stint in a central office job before becoming a superintendent.

In the early 1900s, most superintendents in the United States were white, Protestant, American-born males. Even then, this demographic was not representative of the public school student population (Tyack, 1976). In 1970, there were 11 Black superintendents in the United States (Moody, 1973). Historical information on Asian, Indigenous, and Latine superintendents is minimal. Former superintendent Edward Fort once said, "The most difficult thing about being a Black superintendent is . . . getting the job in the first place" (Moody, 1973, p. 376). The places where they were hired were largely urban, high-poverty, majority-minoritized, and in financial distress and economic turmoil. Looking ahead, Scott (1980) noted that any increase in the number of superintendents of color would not have to do with an interest in diversifying the role but in no one wanting to deal with the "engrossing problems of the cities."

The School Superintendents Association (AASA) reports that the number of superintendents of color is increasing. In their latest survey, they reported that 8.6 percent of respondents identified as superintendents of color in 2020, compared with 6 percent in 2010 and 5 percent in 2000. Nearly 42 percent are women of color (Tienken, 2021).

The challenges of the superintendent who is Asian, Black, Indigenous, Latine, or a person of color remain the same and encompass three areas: (1) access to the role, (2) the economic and social deterioration of the district they are inheriting, and (3) the difficulty in accessing and leveraging the social and political relationships necessary to lead systemic reform within their district, specifically in terms of board relations (Bjork & Kowalski, 2005).

The Equity Officer

Title VII of the Civil Rights Act of 1964 made it unlawful to discriminate against someone based on race, color, national origin, sex (including pregnancy, sexual orientation, and gender identity), or religion. The act also created the Equal Employment Opportunity Commission (EEOC) to enforce Title VII and eliminate unlawful employment discrimination. The EEOC had no power to eliminate any discriminatory practices or to sue or punish any offenders. It was set up only to receive written complaints from individuals who believed they were victims of discrimination.

The chief diversity/equity officer role was born as a response to Title VII. It started in the federal government and then moved to the business sector, healthcare, and higher education. Companies feared getting sued as they were being pressured to diversify. Recently the position has expanded to the K–12 education space, where it adds to the small numbers of leaders of color already in school systems across the United States. As of 2020, 62 percent of the largest 100 districts have a dedicated equity officer, including all of the 10 largest school districts (Greene & Paul, 2021).

As laws, resolutions, and initiatives have passed, the work of implementing them and supporting the groups who need them doesn't fall on the lawmakers who passed them. The work of implementation—sometimes involving community outcry—often leads to the creation of a new office or position, and this position is usually filled by a person of color.

In Boston, the push for integrating schools and busing forced the creation of its first office of equity. Similarly, colleges created roles such as vice president for Black student affairs to respond to the increase in the number of Black students at predominantly white institutions. Particularly since the racial reckoning of 2020, school systems could no longer ignore what history and Asian, Black, Indigenous, Latine, and people of color have been saying for generations: that the school system is a racist institution, and systemic change is necessary in order for the students entering schools every day to be successful.

Williams and Wade-Golden (2007) have characterized the chief equity officer as "a senior administrator who guides, coordinates, leads, enhances, and at times supervises the formal diversity capabilities of the institution in an effort to build sustainable capacity to achieve an environment that is inclusive and excellent for all" (p. 8). They further state:

> Often the position is filled by experienced teachers or administrators with a clear vision of what equity looks like in educational settings. They are disproportionately people of color. They are most likely to be women. Their goals are aligned: support the design and implementation of system-wide equity reforms that will make educational experiences and outcomes more equitable for all students, particularly those who have been minoritized. (Williams & Wade-Golden, 2007, p. 32)

Equity officers are a magnet for criticism. They are seen as the face of a subject that is often sensitive and charged. If their role is well-defined, they must work across all aspects of a school system. There is no formal education for those in this role. There is no professional organization that cuts across higher education, K–12 education, and the corporate and nonprofit sectors (Williams & Wade-Golden, 2007).

Defining the White Space

Today's principals, superintendents, and equity officers face challenges like those that Lucy Laney and Sarah Winnemucca experienced in wanting to create safe spaces for students within a space designed to oppress them. Elijah Anderson (2015) defines "the white space" as the neighborhoods, schools, workplaces, restaurants, and other public spaces that for so long were considered off limits but as a result of the civil rights movement have opened up to Asian, Black, Indigenous, Latine, and other people of color. Some spaces have been quick to integrate; others have taken a while, particularly in regard to leadership roles.

Anderson explains the emotion and feeling of the white space: "The black person's realization of her predicament may be gradual, as awareness often occurs in subtle and ambiguous ways over time, through what may seem to be the deceptively ordinary interactions and negotiations of everyday life" (p. 15). For me, the white space was evident during my schooling to become a principal. I was told by Black graduates of the program I attended that you can be Black but "not too Black." I witnessed that cautionary statement play out as Black classmates were told to cut off their dreads. A fellow Black woman was removed from the program because of her "overtly" Black mannerisms, speech, and language. A colleague of Southeast Asian descent was told to attend "accent reduction" classes. I became aware that to be successful in this white space, I had to be as close to white as possible.

Providing additional description of the white space, Anderson (2015) states:

> In the white space, small issues can become fraught with racial mean-ing or small behaviors can subtly teach or remind the black person of her outsider status, showing onlookers and bystanders alike that she does not really belong, that she is not to be regarded and treated as a full person in the white space. In time, she may conclude that the real problem she faces in this setting is that she is not white and that being white is a fundamental requirement for acceptance and a sense of belonging in the white space. (pp. 15–16)

In my role as equity officer, I facilitated a training during which a white male participant was struggling with the information I was giving him. The feedback to me was that I was too aggressive and hostile. Although I had been brought into the space to facilitate conversations about race, the space wasn't for me. Neither my tone nor my presentation was pal-atable for the participants.

Anti-Blackness and Interracial/Interethnic Relationships

I live in Round Rock, Texas. On my street are families representing countries that include China, the Philippines, India, South Africa, Nigeria, and Mexico. When I walk my son to school every morning, I see many other families walking their kids to school. Some families speak to me; some families don't. I could assume those that don't speak just aren't collegial; I could assume they don't speak to anyone; but I've witnessed the opposite. Anti-blackness is real and isn't just espoused by white people. When proximity to whiteness is your measure of success, your ability to espouse anti-blackness is easy—even if it is directed toward your neighbor.

I wonder if my neighbors recognize that in their efforts, they are doing exactly what white-dominant culture wants. Derald Wing Sue (2015) talks about the "divide-and-conquer" ploy in his book, *Race Talk and the Conspiracy of Silence.* "As long as people fight among themselves, they will be unable to form alliances against systemic forces of racism" (p. 173). Historically, minoritized groups have been pitted against each other for education, employment, and housing. Also at play are the role of colorism and the "oppression Olympics"—the idea that groups need to compete to see who is the most oppressed. All of these factors have led to many interracial conflicts, including between African Americans and Korean Americans during the 1992 Los Angeles protests after the acquittal of police officers charged with beating Rodney King. Other examples include the shooting of African American Trayvon Martin by Latine George Zimmerman and the hate crimes of an African American man against an Asian American woman in the vestibule of an apartment building in New York City in 2021.

These circumstances initially stopped me from wanting to tackle a book focusing on such a vast number of cultures and ethnicities. However, the divide-and-conquer approach has been going on for too long, and there are countless counter-stories that show us what happens when cultures have come together and demonstrated the power of conjoined communities.

The Role of Intersectionality

Intersectionality is the study of how overlapping or intersecting social identities, particularly minoritized identities, relate to systems and structures of oppression, domination, or discrimination (Crenshaw, 1989). Although the foundation of this book is race and the factor that unites the leaders highlighted in it is their racial and ethnic identities, it's important to acknowledge race within the larger context of people's lives, given their multiple identities. In taking a more complex view of culture and cultural oppression, we can examine the realities of those individuals who have been minoritized because of more than one aspect of their demographic background. In the article "Healing Requires Recognition," Bryant-Davis (2007) states that "societal traumas include not only racism but also sexism, poverty, heterosexism, and religious intolerance" (p. 140). Although the stories shared here highlight race and ethnicity, other aspects of each leader's intersectionality are also highlighted to provide a more composite picture.

2

How Do We Stay Here?

[T]he master's tools will never dismantle the master's house.

—Audre Lorde

"Mary, you're a young Black female principal; everything you do matters. Sit at the head of the table and ensure that every move you make, thing you say, makes it clear, you're the leader in this building."

These were the words of my white male coach, a recently retired middle school principal from Brooklyn. At the time, it was difficult for me to embrace the idea that he would be able to give me any advice. However, his words—offered after he had observed me facilitating a meeting—still stay with me.

As I was navigating through the challenge of how to support my 100 percent Black and brown student population, all of whom were undercredited and overage, I was internally battling what it meant to be a Black female principal while consciously not wanting to be labeled the "angry Black woman." I also was building relationships with teachers, some of whom had started teaching the year I was born. I had to recognize my own biases while naming the biases that the teachers had of me.

These internal and interpersonal frictions were all taking place within a school system that was publicly labeling every school with a letter grade and closing struggling schools at an alarming rate. Our small school was battling against a system giving students a very short runway to turn their academic careers around before they were pushed to get their GED.

The expectations and responsibilities of ABILPOC leaders differ from those of their white colleagues. The requirement to be a leader within the cultural community that you represent while also being seen to be a leader of all the communities represented in the district requires a combination of political, emotional, and cultural intelligence that can be exhausting. However, it's not impossible.

Working on the Margins: Dolores Huerta as Role Model

"*Sí se puede! Sí se puede!*" was coined by Dolores Huerta, the cofounder of the National Farm Workers Association. This is how she tells the story:

> We were in Arizona. We were organizing people in the community to come to support us. They had passed a law in Arizona that if you said "boycott," you could go to prison for six months. And if you said "strike," you could go to prison. So we were trying to organize against that law. And I was speaking to a group of professionals in Arizona, to see if they could support us. And they said, "Oh, here in Arizona you can't do any of that. In Arizona *no se puede*—no, you can't." And I said, "No, in Arizona *sí se puede!*" And when I went back to our meeting that we had every night there . . . I gave that report to everybody and when I said, "*Sí se puede*," everybody started shouting, "*Sí se puede! Sí se puede!*" And so that became the slogan of our campaign in Arizona and now is the slogan for the immigrant

rights movement, you know, on posters. We can do it. I can do it. *Sí se puede.* (Godoy, 2017, para. 24)

Dolores Huerta was born in the middle of the Great Depression to Mexican American parents. When she was a student, her teacher accused her of cheating because her papers were too well-written. Despite her own experiences, Dolores became a teacher. However, seeing so many hungry farm children coming to school every day, she thought she could do more to help them by organizing farmers and farmworkers (Michals, 2015).

In 1962, when Huerta cofounded the National Farm Workers Association (NFWA) with activist César Chávez, she took on a role rarely seen by women—particularly Mexican women (Rose, 1990). Reacting to her negotiating style, a representative of the growers said, "Dolores Huerta is crazy. She is a violent woman, where women, especially Mexican women, are usually peaceful and calm" (Rose, 1990, p. 28).

Despite ethnic and gender bias, Huerta was a public figure throughout her work with the NFWA, which later changed its name to the United Farm Workers of America (UFW). Huerta served on the executive board of the UFW and participated in the highest levels of policy-making in the union (Rose, 1990). Her educational background and experience as a teacher gave her self-confidence to speak in front of all types of people. She addressed labor, student, religious, women's, political, antiwar, environmental, and consumer groups. Through print, radio, and television, she raised much-needed funds as well as public awareness of the UFW struggles.

During the 1970s, Huerta became a lobbyist and an advocate on behalf of farmworkers before national, state, and local governmental committees. In appearances before congressional bodies, she argued the union's position on a wide range of issues, from amending migration labor laws to the health problems of field workers to immigration (Rose, 1990). Since the 1990s, she has worked to elect more Latines and women to political office and has championed women's issues (Michals, 2015).

Even with Huerta as a model for what women could do, in June 1969, out of 44 boycott coordinators in major cities, 39 were men and 5 were women. The elevation of those 5 to power was accomplished despite hostile male attitudes toward women with authority (Rose, 1990).

Huerta is another example of what it means to be an ABILPOC leader in your community. This work is not done alone. Just as minoritized communities came together in the 19th century, in the 1960s and 1970s, the Black Panthers, the Chinese American organization known as the Red Guard Party, and the Puerto Rican nationalist group Young Lords were working collectively and individually in their communities but outside the confines of systems and institutions to change behaviors and policies.

The UFW and their allies demonstrated their solidarity in numerous ways. These groups wrote about one another's causes in their newspapers and attended one another's rallies. In California, the Black Panthers and the UFW organizers combined their boycotts of Safeway grocery stores and walked picket lines together. Also in California, Chicano and Japanese American activists demonstrated outside the trial of Black Panther party cofounder Huey Newton. In Chicago, the Panthers and the Young Lords worked together to address poverty and unsafe housing (Araiza, 2013).

What It Takes

Lucy Laney, Sarah Winnemucca, Dolores Huerta, and many others, past and present, took intentional steps to change the life trajectory of the children in their communities. Although they each have diverse intersectional identities, the skills that they leaned on provide today's leaders of color a set of competencies to enact change.

Connecting Leaders of Social Movements and Educational Leaders of Color

A social movement is born from a community need. Cultural and political contexts and societal structures affect the emergence of leaders and movements. The leaders of social movements often change over the arc of the movement, and they are regularly tied to the movement's other members and leaders. Leaders of social movements are effective leaders when they engage participants in discussions about movement ideas and strategies and are actively creating organizations in which participants become involved and new leaders emerge (Morris & Staggenborg, 2004). As educational leaders, we are inextricably linked to the social movements of the past and present, as well as those that will occur in the future. In many social movements, education has been a part of the problem as well as part of the solution. The students, families, and communities we serve every day reveal the gains and disappointments of each social movement.

The skills of social movement leaders can serve leaders of color as well. Research reveals clear connections. Researchers Sharon Nepstad and Clifford Bob (2006) identify three characteristics of effective social movement leaders: (1) cultural capital in the form of knowledge, skills, and abilities that are useful both in the aggrieved community and among external audiences; (2) social capital embodied in strong ties to activist communities and weak ties to broader mobilizing networks; and (3) symbolic capital, including charisma, that reflects respect, social prestige, and moral authority.

Ganz (2000) identifies several features of organizations that generate effective leaders and increase their ability to embody the three characteristics laid out by Nepstad and Bob. First, organizations that create "regular, open, and authoritative deliberation" give leaders access to information and the authority to act on decisions. Second, "organizations that mobilize resources from multiple constituencies" give leaders flexibility. Last, organizations that hold leaders accountable to their constituents are likely to have leaders with useful knowledge and political skills. Ganz also argues that it is the "leadership team" rather than an individual leader that collectively possesses these skills within an organization providing the support.

Other Standards of Influence

The Professional Standards for Educational Leaders developed by the National Policy Board for Educational Administration consists of

10 standards (2015). Standard #3 speaks to equity and cultural responsiveness. However, Davis and colleagues (2015) conclude that following these standards will not result in an equity-focused leader, nor do the standards take into consideration the nuances of being an ABILPOC leader.

The National Association of Diversity Officers in Higher Education has created 16 standards of professional practice for chief diversity officers. All the standards speak explicitly to the work on a college campus (Worthington et al., 2020). The competencies developed by Williams and Wade-Golden (2007) are also built on their studies of diversity officers on college campuses.

The competencies I present in the next section draw from a combination of my research on leaders of social movements, my analysis of the experiences of K–12 equity officers, and my own experiences. They differ from the previously mentioned standards and competencies in that they do the following:

- Consider the tensions of being a person of color leading within white spaces.
- Are based on the experiences of K–12 education leaders, although they can be applied universally.
- Break down the competencies of a leader through the lens of individual, interpersonal, and institutional moves.
- Are built on the premise of collectivism versus individualism.

The Competencies

Here are the competencies that leaders can employ to lead within spaces of inequity and create a new system:

1. Demonstrate self-awareness.
2. Operate outside your comfort zone.
3. Practice love and rage.
4. Practice self-care.
5. Engage in authentic dialogue.
6. Attend to relationships.

7. Create a coalition.
8. Be patient but persistent.
9. Take a stand in pursuit of a liberatory education system even if it's unpopular.
10. Act to change systemic racism every day in policies, procedures, and systems.

The competencies are divided into three categories. Competencies 1 through 4 are *individual*; 5 through 7 are *interpersonal*; and 8 through 10 are *institutional*. They are distinct but interconnected. This interconnection recognizes that ABILPOC leaders are responsible for navigating oppressions on these three levels.

I was first introduced to these lenses of oppression through the National Equity Project. This nonprofit organization describes *individual oppressions* as exhibiting behaviors such as explicit and implicit bias as well as experiencing stereotype threat and internalized oppression. *Interpersonal oppression* includes microaggressions, racist interactions, and transferred oppression. Finally, *institutional oppression* includes biased policies and practices (e.g., in hiring, teaching, discipline, parent-family engagement) and disproportional (e.g., racialized) outcomes and experiences (National Equity Project, 2012).

In her book *Culturally Responsive Teaching and the Brain*, Zaretta Hammond (2015) explains that our brains are wired to be in community. We naturally gravitate toward cooperation and togetherness, which is how most cultures operate. Unfortunately, most European cultures operate in an individualistic culture, which has become the dominant culture (Hammond, 2015).

We have all seen individualism play out in our school and work experience. We may also assume the value of, and believe in, self-reliance and the notion that a person is supposed to take care of themselves to get ahead. We may hold on to the ideal that individual contributions and status are important. These learned behaviors and beliefs are why the competencies here are offered in an individualistic frame, as we are leading in the individualistic framework of the United States education system.

However, collectivism is where we deliberately shift away from dominant culture. Collectivism emphasizes reliance on the collective wisdom or resources of the group and the belief that group members take care of each other to get ahead. In a collectivist culture, group dynamics and harmony are important (Hammond, 2015). Although the competencies are presented as individual actions, growth and learning in their execution are achieved by being in community with others. Each competency is grounded in the importance of community and in alignment to the cultures that we come from as leaders of color.

We will explore the competencies in detail in the upcoming chapters, but see Figure 2.1 for a brief overview of each of them, why they are important, what they look like in practice, and how, when practiced, they deliberately dismantle white-dominant culture.

A Continuum of Competency Development

The purpose of presenting a continuum of competency development (Figure 2.2) is to show a progression of learning while also showing that learning is never over. Unlike a typical rubric, the continuum has no "mastery" or "exemplary" category. Often people like to use the marathon-versus-sprint metaphor to explain leadership in a school system. Unfortunately, as a marathoner myself, this metaphor just doesn't work for me. When running a marathon, I know the end point. At 26.2 miles, the running will be over. I can stop, breathe, and celebrate. However, the end point of competency development is not clear. If you are looking to create a school system that is built for students, staff, and families that embody your intersectional identities, the end point may not come in your lifetime. Although this continuum gives you some guidance, don't expect to hit mastery—ever.

FIGURE 2.1

An Overview of the 10 Competencies

Competency	The Competency's Importance to an ABILPOC Leader	How to Embody the Competency	How the Competency Is an Antidote to White-Dominant Culture*
Individual			
1. Demonstrate self-awareness.	Socialization has led us to internalize and act in ways that only continue to oppress the oppressed unless we interrogate ourselves.	• Know yourself. • Embrace healing.	It prevents us from trying to adhere to what it means to be "qualified" in any setting.
2. Operate outside your comfort zone.	Being intimately aware of our double-consciousness will provide us with the ability to stretch.	• Meet your fear. • Make the work your own.	It moves us away from the belief that we have a "right to comfort."
3. Practice love and rage.	We need to embrace these emotions, which are foundational to revolutionary change.	• Focus on action. • Redefine the trope.	It minimizes the "fear" that dominant culture uses to disconnect us from each other and ourselves.
4. Practice self-care.	Generational trauma is a real thing. We need to be right within ourselves so we can lead others.	• Practice physical self-care. • Practice mental self-care. • Practice spiritual self-care.	It takes away the blame and shame associated with "individualism" when needing to take care of ourselves.
Interpersonal			
5. Engage in authentic dialogue.	Engaging in cross-difference conversations can be emotionally exhausting, especially when speaking to someone who is part of the dominant culture. Dialogue is effective when recognizing the vulnerability, historical distrust, and risk demanded of conversations regarding race.	• Agree to disagree. • See the whole person. • Educate. • Ask questions. • Share your experiences. • Use a framework.	It provides skill sets to engage with others who have a "fear of open conflict" and others who exhibit "defensiveness" during conversations.

Competency	The Competency's Importance to an ABILPOC Leader	How to Embody the Competency	How the Competency Is an Antidote to White-Dominant Culture*
6. Attend to relationships.	We did not create this oppressive society, so we alone cannot and should not try to dismantle it. Relationships are beneficial when we embrace coconspirators across race, culture, and perspectives.	• Show humanity and humility. • Set explicit intentions. • Choose wisely.	It moves away from "individualist" concepts that we should make it on our own and pull ourselves up by our own bootstraps.
7. Create a coalition.	A coalition of liberatory leaders that generates communal wisdom and problem solving is part of our culture.	• Have a clear objective. • Think beyond yourself. • Manage political landmines. • Add layers. • Create more than one coalition.	It eliminates the value placed on "power hoarding" and the "paternalistic" belief that those who hold official power should be the sole decision makers.
Institutional			
8. Be patient but persistent.	The education system will push for quick reform/fixes and only push what they know versus what will ensure progress. Know it will take time to create new liberatory education systems.	• Give the "why." • Avoid getting trapped. Focus on policy.	It deliberately attacks the need for "urgency" connected to every initiative and the push for "perfectionism" in every action.
9. Take a stand in pursuit of a liberatory education system even if it's unpopular.	Our perspectives, experiences, and divergent thinking may differ from others within or close to white-dominant culture.	• Stay connected to the community. • Be systematic. • Always be a teacher. • Recognize that intersectionality matters.	It minimizes the belief that the goal is to be neutral and to assume "objectivity."
10. Act to change systemic racism every day in policies, procedures, and systems.	We will be distracted from changing systems that benefit dominant culture and that are seen as "untouchable."	• Center students and families. • Fight systems with systems. • Stay true to your values.	It is counter to the idea that there is "one right way" to creating a liberatory education system.

* Each characteristic comes from "White Supremacy Culture—Still Here" (Okun, 2021).

FIGURE 2.2

A Continuum of Competency Development

Competency	Starting to Learn	Regularly Learning	Still Learning and Growing
Individually			
1. Demonstrate self-awareness.	Taking steps to reflect on the impacts of your upbringing.	Semiregularly interrogating your upbringing and current actions. Have taken initial steps to deliberately heal from traumatic experiences related to intersectional identities.	Consistently interrogating yourself to not take on the role of the oppressor. Embracing healing as a regular act of understanding the role of socialization in how you lead.
2. Operate outside your comfort zone.	Building skill sets to move away from what is personally comfortable.	Practicing skill sets to operate in a space outside your comfort zone.	Actively moving away from what is comfortable for you. Choosing connections as a tool to gravitate toward the unknown.
3. Practice love and rage.	Identifying when you are feeling the emotions of love and rage.	Tapping into emotions to engage with others.	Leaning into the emotions of love and rage to create space to express yourself, and calling out issues of inequity and opportunities for liberation.
4. Practice self-care.	Practicing being physically, mentally, or spiritually right within yourself but have yet to establish a routine or habit.	Regularly practicing being physically, mentally, or spiritually right within yourself. Learning to exhibit love to a variety of stakeholders.	Practicing with a balanced approach to be physically, mentally, and spiritually right within yourself so you can show love for others.
Interpersonally			
5. Engage in authentic dialogue.	Using one primary strategy to engage in authentic conversations about race, with inconsistent results.	Using a limited number of strategies (agree to disagree, see the whole person, educate, ask questions, share your experiences, use a framework) to engage in authentic conversations about race.	Regularly engaging in authentic conversations about race using a variety of strategies (agree to disagree, see the whole person, educate, ask questions, share your experiences, use a framework) that will allow others to recognize their past, present, and future.

6. Attend to relationships.	Forming relationships across difference that provide some new perspectives, but depth and breadth are limited.	Forming relationships across difference that provide some new perspectives.	Actively building intentional relationships with explicit intentions across difference that widen your perspective.
7. Create a coalition.	Coalition is forming and is part of the conversation but is not part of the decision making.	Coalition is established and bringing diverse perspectives, but agency and power are limited.	Consistently centering the diverse coalition that will collaboratively manage political landmines and collectively create a plan of action.

Institutionally

8. Be patient but persistent.	Identifying focused tasks, but the tasks are minimized due to urgency associated with other initiatives.	Identifying focused tasks and implementing with deliberate pacing.	Actively consistent and focused on the tasks that create liberatory education systems by constantly trying, evaluating, and retrying.
9. Take a stand in pursuit of a liberatory education system even if it's unpopular.	Being inconsistent in sharing perspectives and leaning toward trying to be neutral or objective during decision making.	Semiregularly being vocal in what needs to happen to create a liberatory education system.	Regularly taking the perspective that will bring about the drastic change necessary to create a liberatory education system by staying connected to the community, being systemic, and understanding the importance and role of intersectionality.
10. Act to change systemic racism every day in policies, procedures, and systems.	Pushing for change in the system but may be focusing on only mindsets and bias versus policy, and may be providing only one solution.	Regularly pushing for change in the system using multiple options, including bias and policy changes.	Actively using every day as an opportunity to push to change the education system beyond mindsets and bias, to the level where systems are dismantled and updated to meet the needs of current student populations.

3

Looking Inward

Simply being a victim does not radicalize your consciousness.

—bell hooks

"Are you coachable?" That was the interview question Janice K. Jackson, the CEO of Chicago Public Schools (CPS), asked Maurice Swinney when he was applying to become the district's first chief equity officer.

As a Black male leader in the third-largest school district in the country, Maurice understood that he needed to bring all his previous experiences to the table, but to make a difference, he needed to be able to be sure of who he was and willing to discover new things about himself along the way.

Maurice came into the role as a reflective leader and continues his reflection while engaging and interacting with others within and outside the school system. One example of this approach occurred during the process of developing the CPS Equity Framework. The process included hearing from students, families, community members, and CPS staff. In collecting the perspectives of so many different community members, Maurice heard from many people of color who were demanding immediate change. But with further reflection, he understood that "people really want to be included and see their voices impacting something while it's being constructed, which creates a space of safety and makes it OK for something not to be immediate. But if you're not going to listen to me, then I'm going to demand that it happens right now."

The importance of reflection and looking inward is central to the CPS Equity Framework. The work of the individual is explained using the acronym "CURVE," which stands for the following behaviors:

- *C—Withhold judgment and be in a space of inquiry—be **curious** to gain a better understanding of an issue.*
- *U—Work with a sense of **urgency** when championing the success of our students. We have to respond in a timely manner.*
- *R—Acknowledge that this work can be difficult and requires **resiliency**.*
- *V—Recognize that each of us may not know a solution, but we can be **vulnerable** to collectively learn and problem-solve together.*
- *E—Build connection. Show **empathy** across differences, with someone who you think may not share your experiences. (Chicago Public Schools, n.d.)*

The CURVE is a tool for individuals to use to reflect on their disposition and to support communication. Maurice explains that it is intended to allow CPS employees to ground themselves, look inward, and recognize where they are in any conversation.

He continues to have moments when he is personally leaning into the CURVE to see how he is engaging with the students, adults, and communities he interacts with every day. He shares that every time he meets a new group of people, he takes a step back and asks himself, "Maurice, how do you begin to show up in these spaces as a person who is listening and attentive to other people's needs while being very honest about your experiences and how you're showing up?"

He also supports the inward reflections of others. He explains, "When I talk to people of color, the conversation centers on what their healing and transformation work looks like and what might the changes be." He encourages others to turn the mirror on themselves so that they can learn something they don't already know.

Maurice believes people must have true affinity spaces for themselves—different from the "watercooler conversation." When you are in true community with others, you can say, "Here's what I'm wrestling with. I'm wondering how people are experiencing me in this way."

To Be Young, Gifted, and Black: Lorraine Hansberry as Role Model

The city, neighborhoods, and streets that Maurice Swinney travels every day are the same that shaped the life of Lorraine Hansberry many decades before. Hansberry was born in 1930, the youngest of four children in a Black middle-class family on the South Side of Chicago. In her short 34 years on this earth, Lorraine Hansberry did not just give us her award-winning play *A Raisin in the Sun*. Her experiences and her decisions gave us insights into what it means to be conscious of the impacts of socialization on ourselves and those around us and how to consciously connect with others.

Her mother, a teacher, and her father, a real estate entrepreneur, socialized her to be a good reflection of the race but in a manner that would be respectable to white and other affluent Black people. Her parents did challenge racism, particularly redlining, by integrating a white neighborhood in Chicago, but their action was attached to patriotic ideals of American capitalism (Perry, 2018).

When she attended one of the first integrated high schools in Chicago, her nice clothes helped her to assimilate, and she showed no desire to ruffle any feathers among the white students who didn't want Black kids there. She was successful in high school and could have easily continued on the path created for her by her parents and attended a historically Black college or university; however, she decided to follow a different path (Perry, 2018).

Through her short time at the University of Wisconsin–Madison and her move to New York City, Hansberry removed the veil given to her by her parents and built her own perspectives on those different from her. Her mentors, activist and historian W. E. B. Du Bois and singer and actor Paul Robeson, gave her insights into communism and a different perspective on the United States. She also befriended singer Nina Simone and writers James Baldwin and Langston Hughes. They provided refuge and peace to one another while pushing each other to use their voices as a platform.

Hansberry also became personally in touch with her sexuality and engaged in relationships with women. "It is unquestionable that her desire for women and her love of women was meaningful as part of her politics, her intellectual life, and her aesthetics, as well as her spirit" (Perry, 2018, p. 79). At the same time, she married a white Jewish musician and learned to navigate a New York City hostile to interracial couples.

In her private journals, Hansberry shared concerns that she was becoming a coward. "Do I remain a revolutionary?" she wrote. "Intellectually—without a doubt. But am I prepared to give my body to the struggle or even my comforts? . . . Comfort has come to be its own corruption" (Nemiroff & Hansberry, 1970, pp. 249–250). Later she wrote that when she regained her health (she had been diagnosed with pancreatic cancer), she might travel to the South "to find out what kind of revolutionary I am."

"Sweet Lorraine," by James Baldwin, is the introduction to Hansberry's memoir, *To Be Young, Gifted, and Black*, published after her death. In it, Baldwin describes how Hansberry navigated her unpacking of herself:

> She was wise enough and honest enough to recognize that black American artists are a very special case. . . . To continue to grow, to remain in touch with himself, he needs the support of that community from which, however, all of the pressures of American life incessantly conspire to remove him. . . . Much of the strain under which Lorraine

worked was produced by her knowledge of this reality, and her determined refusal to be destroyed by it. (Baldwin, 1969, pp. xviii, xix)

Imani Perry, author of *Looking for Lorraine,* summarizes Hansberry as a person and as an activist in the final paragraph of the biography:

The battles Lorraine fought are still before us: exploitation of the poor, racism, neocolonialism, homophobia, and patriarchy. She models some of what we must do to confront them: use frank speech, beauty, imagination, and courage. And be with the people. (Perry, 2018, p. 200)

Competency 1: Demonstrate Self-Awareness

We are born without bias, assumptions, or questions, but that circumstance quickly changes. To demonstrate self-awareness is to be constantly aware of what has led you to internalize whiteness. Maurice Swinney and Lorraine Hansberry demonstrate this in their lived experiences. The cycle of socialization imposes acceptable ways of being that often bring harm and oppression. Socialization has also led us to continue to oppress the oppressed unless we interrogate ourselves (Harro, 2000).

Harro's five stages of socialization—the beginning, first socialization, institutional and cultural socialization, enforcements, and results—unpack what socialization is and how it works. "The beginning" stage is when we are born, with no blame, no guilt, and no consciousness; however, there are already societal norms set in place.

The second stage is the "first socialization," during which we are learning from those we love and trust how we should behave and act. Although we have no say regarding what any of our intersectional identities will be when we are born, there is a dominant culture that we are born into, and this affects us from our very first day of existence. In my case, I grew up in Wisconsin, and my parents followed Southern Baptist principles. My mother believed children should be "seen, not heard." This meant we were spotlessly dressed, minded our manners, and were never to ask for anything in a store or talk back. This socialization was a result of the church values my parents believed in but was also a direct result of my Black parents being born and raised in the segregated South. They were teaching me survival skills.

In addition to the socialization from my parents, there was also "institutional and cultural socialization," which can come from school and church as well as television and popular music. In my younger years, I spent a lot of time engaged in church activities and attended a Christian school, so my thoughts were formulated by how the adults around me interpreted and taught what they believed the Bible said. A repeated Sunday school song had the lyric "red and yellow, black or white, they are precious in His sight." The church was teaching color blindness, but I was also attending the predominantly white institutions of school. In kindergarten, I quickly noticed that all the Black kids in the class were relegated to the lowest-level reading groups. I knew no one had tested my reading. The institution of school taught me that race matters.

The fourth stage, "enforcements," occurs when you are rewarded for staying within societal norms or punished when you step outside them. In my case, I was rewarded for "being so well-spoken" and fitting in with the rest of the kids in my classes but greeted with shock and confusion when I spoke out against the celebration of Columbus Day with no recognition of Martin Luther King Jr. Day during my high school years.

The fifth and final stage is "results"—the outcome of the cycle, which can manifest itself in different ways. It can lead to anger and dissonance in those who see the discrepancy between what the United States stands for and what happens daily in the lives of its citizens. Internalizing these emotions can lead to feeling helpless or perpetuating oppression.

The actions taken after the final stage of socialization are important. They can include doing nothing, not making any waves, and continuing to promote the status quo. These actions were my first response when I entered the workforce as a teacher. As I reflect on this cycle, I recognize that my actions resulted from fear, insecurity, and ignorance. I wanted to do well and keep my job, but I was not paying attention to how I was reinforcing this cycle with my Black and brown students.

However, the "direction for change" (Harro, 2000) involves interrupting, raising consciousness, and taking a stand. For me, this turn came when I understood the connection between power and oppression and how it is manifested in institutions. I saw how little impact I was making for the students I was serving because my own eyes were not open to the layers of oppression that I had internalized. So I had to do my own reflections and unlearning to become an advocate for myself and my students.

How to Demonstrate Self-Awareness

When I engage leaders in going through their own cycle of socialization process, I say, "There's only one Mary Rice-Boothe, and that's the lens which I look through everything." This is true and problematic. Deliberatively widening my lens in all instances and interactions is a muscle that I am still working on. To widen that lens requires the following behaviors: knowing yourself and embracing healing.

Know Yourself

We ABILPOC leaders require a level of self-awareness that allows us to be clear about what we are called to do, what we know how to do, and where we need to develop. The cycle of socialization means we have internalized cultural messages about our worth and often act on those messages without realizing we are doing so. We also tend to reproduce white-dominant cultural habits, such as assuming the right to comfort. Knowing ourselves means taking responsibility for our actions, inactions, and how we show up to facilitate forward movement.

Lisa is a Black equity officer in a large district in Virginia. She talked about what this effort looked like for her:

> I did work around understanding whiteness, understanding internalization of whiteness, understanding anti-blackness, internalization of anti-blackness, liberatory work, self-care work. I think through all of that, it was an unlearning process. And not so much unlearning to the point of, I felt, feeling like there are parts of myself that I had to get rid of, but there were more parts of myself that I needed to reclaim.

What this effort meant for Lisa is what it means for me as a Black woman and for others. We need to notice that we are often taught to not love certain parts of ourselves, but the things we are taught to not love are the most sacred things about us.

Stephen, a Vietnamese American equity officer at a nonprofit in California, spoke about the impact on him of the cycle of socialization:

> I come from a family of Vietnamese refugees who came here in 1975 and very much believed in the American dream and code-switched— learned how to code-switch very quickly into professional spaces and white spaces, essentially. So that was kind of passed on to me, and I thought that was how we needed to operate to be successful.

This recognition of assimilation pushed Stephen in his journey toward self-awareness. As he recounted:

> I've really interrogated my identity and my upbringing, and how that affects my success in the workplace and in this role, specifically, of how to really shift my mindset to thinking about how I live authentically and really own who I am.

In their comments, both Lisa and Stephen are speaking to the desire to want to fit in, to be part of white-dominant culture, and have pinpointed where whiteness has been a part of every level of their interactions and consciousness, including basic rights, values, beliefs, perspectives, and experiences. This is the feeling described by W. E. B. Du Bois as "this double-consciousness, this sense of always looking at oneself through the eyes of others, of measuring one's soul by the tape of a world that looks on in amused contempt and pity" (Du Bois, 1897, p. 5).

Embrace Healing

As an ABILPOC leader, you may have experienced trauma from the white-dominant culture that you grew up in. In unpacking and uncovering the socialization you experienced, you will need to create a space for healing. Healing may involve one-on-one therapy for some, but collective healing is also a process to connect individuals with a community.

Danielle is a Black equity officer in a large district in Florida. She shared the hurt she has felt and the healing she has done since taking on this role:

> As a Black woman, I find it difficult for me at times to assume the role as the leader of this work but also know how it currently feels to be marginalized. In my K–12 years, I've always felt a victim to not knowing my full history, so thinking about where I've missed opportunities for real understanding of African American history as a kid, to not seeing others like me well-represented in school as students, teachers, guidance counselors, or leadership at the schools. But now being in a K–12 leader role, I still feel those moments of feeling like a victim and wanting to share victim-like experiences with my peers and with the students today, but also understand that my goal as a leader is to acknowledge those experiences as examples to focus on making changes to the culture of our schools through empathy and healing.

Danielle's observations speak to how she was able to pinpoint the trauma she may have experienced and to recognize the importance of being right with herself before engaging in working with others.

Mariane, a female African immigrant equity officer in a medium-size district in California, expressed how her experiences and healing bring a heightened level of empathy for her to do her work:

> I've lived in my car. I had to drop out of high school to work full-time and pursue my college education. I think because we happen to be women, people of color, immigrants—because we have all those things—we also then had all these other experiences that we didn't want to have, but we had them. Perhaps that helped us develop a deeper sense of empathy.

The trauma has brought empathy, but staying in a place of trauma won't sustain them or the work they are committed to leading. Michael is a Black equity officer in a large district in Tennessee. He spoke about how knowing himself has led to healing: "I've learned a lot; I have to be what I need to be for the students that I serve but also letting people know—you got to be comfortable being yourself."

Healing may also be a physical process. In *My Grandmother's Hands,* author Resmaa Menakem (2017) talks about the "soul nerve." He describes it as "where you experience a felt sense of love, compassion, fear, grief, dread, sadness, loneliness, hope, empathy, anxiety, caring, disgust, despair, and many other things that make us human" (p. 139). The book provides exercises so individuals can learn to work with their soul nerve—consciously and deliberately relaxing their muscles, settling their body, and soothing themselves during difficult or high-stress situations.

Competency 2: Operate Outside Your Comfort Zone

To operate outside your comfort zone is to actively move away from what is comfortable for you and to gravitate toward the unknown. In her 2014 TEDxBeaconStreet Talk, diversity advocate Verna Myers looked closely at some of the subconscious attitudes we hold toward others whose identities differ from our own. She provided several suggestions for those looking to unpack and minimize their biases. One suggestion was to "move toward, not away from, the groups that make you uncomfortable." This suggestion highlighted in the talk was connected to talking to young Black men, but in an interview she explained that this advice is for everyone:

> This is something that every human being has to deal with. It's not like, "White people have to deal with this, and black people don't." All of us have a comfort zone. My observation is: In the hopes of being respectful and sensitive, people create distance between themselves and people they don't know well. The only remedy for that is to get to know people. So look for opportunities to extend the connection that you do have with people of difference. Get a little bit closer and go deeper. Listen longer in a conversation, be more curious about what people's views are, share your own life with them. Instead of just, "Hi," and keeping it neat, really lean into the conversation and be curious about what you don't know. And be okay about sharing your own worldview. (Ha, 2014, para. 2)

She continued to explain for introverts and others less comfortable:

> Get curious. Don't do things out of guilt or shame—that rarely actually shifts things, because you get paternalistic or condescending. Be curious; read; notice, notice, notice. Ask open-ended questions instead of questions that have embedded assumptions about people. (Ha, 2014, para. 13)

I consider myself an introvert. The idea of walking up to a stranger and starting small talk is an activity that will always be on the bottom of my list of fun things to do. Then to walk up to a stranger whose experiences and differences are different from my own, adding to the probability of offending and misspeaking? Doing that was initially a challenge. Then I thought about the fact that I have always been a reader, and my early reading was fiction. The characters and places described in the books were different from my experience. The Nancy Drew series, the Boxcar Children series, *Anne of Green Gables*—I read them all. By the time I entered middle school, I knew more about the cultures and histories of others than my own. At the same time I was reading, I was also asking questions. It may have come from being the youngest child or the disconnects I saw between my life and the books I was reading, but I never stopped asking *why*? This curiosity drives me to the unknown.

However, the challenge with Myers's suggestion of moving toward what makes you uncomfortable is that it is counter to the white-supremacy characteristics of having the "right to comfort" that many of us as professionals with privilege lean into regularly. Now, this is not to say that as an ABILPOC leader in a school system, you aren't daily taking a risk by showing up. We are expected to take risks and manage the consequences. However, as we have progressed in our careers, we have acquired privilege and comfort.

Tema Okun and Kenneth Jones (2001) presented their characteristics of white-supremacist culture as part of their Dismantling Racism workshop to help individuals and organizations identify what might be getting in the way of their journey to becoming equitable organizations and presented antidotes to address the harmful actions. In 2021, Okun updated these characteristics. She describes the "right to comfort" as presenting itself through the following:

- The belief that those with power have a right to emotional and psychological comfort (another aspect of valuing "logic" over emotion);
- Scapegoating those who cause discomfort, for example, targeting and isolating those who name racism rather than addressing the actual racism that is being named;
- Demanding, requiring, expecting apologies or other forms of "I didn't mean it" when faced with accusations of colluding with racism;
- Feeling entitled to name what is and isn't racism;
- White people (or those with dominant identities) equating individual acts of unfairness with systemic racism (or other forms of oppression). (Okun, 2021, p. 25)

But to operate outside your comfort zone, your mindset needs to shift. You need to see discomfort as a gift. Okun offers the following "antidotes" to support this transition:

- Understand that discomfort is at the root of all growth and learning;
- Welcome discomfort and learn to sit with discomfort before responding or acting;
- Deepen your political analysis of racism and oppression so you have a strong understanding of how your personal experience and feelings fit into a larger picture;
- Avoid taking everything personally;
- Welcome honest and hard feedback as the gift it is, knowing that people could so easily choose to stay silent and talk about you behind your back rather than gift you with their truth about how your attitudes and/or behavior are causing a problem;
- When you have a different point of view, seek to understand what you're being told and assume there is a good reason for what is being said; seek to find and understand that good reason (without labeling the other person);

- Remember that feedback and criticism may be skillful or unskillful and either way, it will not kill you;
- Remember that critical feedback can help you see your conditioning as you learn to separate your conditioning from who you actually are; you need to know your conditioning if you are going to be free; while your conditioning is hazardous, you are not. (Okun, 2021, p. 25)

How to Operate Outside Your Comfort Zone

No matter the results of your Myers-Briggs, DISC, or True Colors test, operating outside your comfort zone is critical to achieving liberation. This can be done by meeting your fear and making the work your own.

Meet Your Fear

Fear is a part of our everyday culture. The impact of fear is division, and it limits our ability to be compassionate and courageous. Being in tune when fear is present and choosing to build relationships and connections is a part of being able to move outside your comfort zone. Ground your actions in connection, even if first with yourself. In 1957, Martin Luther King Jr. delivered the sermon "The Mastery of Fear." In it he talks about how fear is a part of our everyday life as well as a reason for the racial division within the United States. However, he doesn't believe that we should get rid of fear. Instead, he says, "We must harness it and master it" (King, 2007).

Monica is an Afro-Latina equity officer in a large district in Florida. She shared the following about how to embrace uncomfortable connection over fear:

> I think you need to be in tune with your core beliefs, values. Because if you really are not willing to push things and fight for things, you're probably, number one, not going to be comfortable in the role, and not going to be successful in the role. I'm in a place in my life where I'm not operating in fear; I'm operating in faith.

She went on to explain: "If you are not making people uncomfortable, you're probably not making anything happen." This equity officer has used her "faith over fear" approach to talk to the numerous communities within her district to hear their concerns. She has taken the time to meet one-on-one with leaders in the community, which has helped her build connection and the conditions to be able to operate in a space of discomfort.

My antidote to fear is to first recognize it as the primary emotion that I am feeling and then to name it. Once I accept the emotion, I can take a variety of measures to move past it. For example, I wear something red, which I see as my "power color." A whole section of my closet consists of red apparel. When I know I am going to be walking into a meeting, conversation, or space where fear may come up, I make sure I am wearing red. Your antidotes may be different, but we each must develop skills to meet our fear, name it, and work to avoid letting it drive our actions and decisions.

Make the Work Your Own

Andy Molinsky is a professor of organizational behavior and international management at Brandeis University. His work helps people step outside their personal and cultural comfort zones. He explains that very few people struggle in every type of situation. His advice is that you find the space to make a situation work for you. One example he provides is someone who hates public speaking. He suggests that instead of avoiding public speaking altogether, "look for opportunities to speak with smaller groups or set up intimate coffee meetings with those you want to network with" (Molinsky, 2016, para. 5).

Gilmara, a Latina equity officer in a medium-size district in Iowa, shared how knowing herself led her to embrace conflict:

> What I have learned about myself at the beginning as a young professional was that I needed to embrace conflict a little, if I wanted to be effective in this role. Because the resistance and the pushback were going to be present, not only because of the nature of the work of being so emotionally charged, but also controversial for some people. But also, as an immigrant, a person with an accent, a woman, a woman of color, all the intersectionality of all these identity markers positioned

me in a way that I would encounter even more resistance. And so I learned how to navigate and embrace conflict and push back really intentionally.

Laurice, a biracial equity officer in a small district in Wisconsin, also shared how she became comfortable with a new approach:

One of the things that I really have learned is just being OK with the nonclosure of the work in a day-to-day, encounter-to-encounter space. Understanding this is just the work and it's always going to be a journey and that's OK.

She went on to explain:

So when I'm in the day-to-day encounters, I think for me I can walk away from something, and I've learned how to disconnect the emotional piece in that moment and know that there's going to be another moment.

I've gotten comfortable with just naming it. Doing so is what I need in order to do this work from both a personal and a professional standpoint. Many times, I address it in the moment. However, I'm a slow processor, and sometimes, when a comment is said in the moment, I don't process its impact right away. If something is said in a conversation and I'm still thinking about it 24 hours later, I come back to it. As these equity officers shared, their self-awareness led them to find an approach that worked best for them while also continuing, every day, to push the conversation and the work.

Conclusion

In the integrated model of racial identity development, Rabow (2014) states that getting to the place of "integrative awareness" is when ABILPOC arrive to the fact that there is much more to them than their race or gender. They positively identify with their own racial group while also acknowledging that other aspects of their identity are equally important to who they are as an individual.

Although we may get to the place of "integrative awareness," we rarely stay there. Many of us have spent many years learning how to assimilate and being rewarded for our ability to do so. Unlearning it all can be overwhelming—especially when you're working within a system that is pushing you to assimilate. Intentionally knowing and seeing where you are upholding the white-dominant culture and at the same time intentionally replacing it with antidotes that will center you and your own voice is a necessary healing experience.

Key Takeaways

- As an ABILPOC leader, you first need to be right with yourself, your history, and your emotions. Be willing to unpack your cycle of socialization and reflect on the stories that made you.
- Once you understand yourself, you need to deliberately learn about others—particularly those whose experiences differ from your own. Engage with communities, organizations, and individuals that will provide learning for you as well as for them.
- Discomfort is a necessary state for ABILPOC leaders, but you can make it your own. Try out a variety of strategies that will help you lean into that discomfort.

"Taking It Further" Reflection Questions

- Using the cycle of socialization, unpack your experiences growing up. What did you learn about yourself?
- What actions can you take to go from a "right to comfort" to seeing discomfort as a gift?
- Instead of turning toward fear, ask yourself, "What would build connection here? What would build relationship? What would build love?"

Additional Resources

- In *Shifting: The Double Lives of Black Women in America*, Charisse Jones and Kumea Shorter-Gooden (2003) discuss the pressure that African American women feel to adapt to their circumstances.

- In *For Brown Girls with Sharp Edges and Tender Hearts: A Love Letter to Women of Color,* Prisca Dorcas Mojica Rodríguez (2021) provides tools and direction for women of color to tell their own stories and create their own path toward liberation.
- In *I Hope We Choose Love: A Trans Girl's Notes from the End of the World,* a collection of personal essays and prose poems, Kai Cheng Thom (2019) discusses how social movements can continue to move forward and create a better future.

4

Practicing Love, Rage, and Self-Care

I must undertake to love myself and to respect myself as though my very life depends upon self-love and self-respect.

—June Jordan

"The major goal that I have is collective consciousness, because you can't change what you can't see."

That statement is from Lisa Williams, who came to Fairfax Public Schools in Virginia as chief equity officer with more than a decade of experience in a similar role. She knew what it looked like to "skirt around the edges" of equity. She knew that this role and district needed more than just celebrations and professional development to see itself as an equitable school district, and she embraced the challenge.

Her experience told her that a large district working at a high-speed pace was not set up for individuals and groups to be reflective and creative enough to do something different. They had to slow down and tell a different story so the organization could wake up and become aware of its own conditions. The story she presented was not just one of closing academic gaps. It included her revealing structural patterns. She explains, "The lack of opportunity in AP is the same lack of opportunity in contractual positions, is the same lack of opportunity that bus drivers have. There are these patterns that, irrespective of what you're talking about, you see the same pattern."

Lisa has recognized that once the patterns within the story are seen, her team can focus on collective impact across offices. They are the consciousness of the organization, which means that they all have to do their own personal work to figure out the most pressing issues of equity, access, and institutional racism.

This level of storytelling requires a different level of data analysis, which has been a personal choice for Lisa as well. She explains:

> I try to spend most of my time being the most compelling because I am the most dialed in and present. I'm showing up as my best self. So, my best self understands the data, not just in a one-dimensional way, but how it is embodied, how it walks, how it talks, how you present it in a written form. That's my best self. And when I'm doing that, it is more likely that I'm going to have fewer of these folks who don't want to slow down and see.

To foster and lead this approach to dismantling inequitable practices and creating new ones, Lisa has been intentional about how she practices love and self-care. Physically, she is a regular runner who ensures she gets enough to drink. Spiritually, she has a meditative practice focused on setting and maintaining boundaries. Mentally, she has intentionally engaged in liberatory work that has given her the ability to take a stance. "I just decided to be me and be less worried about what was going to happen on the other end of that," she says.

A centerpiece of Lisa's self-love and self-care is her tight circle of friends. She intentionally minimizes the amount of time she spends with folks she doesn't want to be around and has curated a friendship circle in a particular way. She explains:

My friendship circle is a circle of people who are conscious. It is just a different kind of beauty. There's a lot of Black women because I need to be in the company of people who understand that lived experience. But my white friends know how to deploy their whiteness on my behalf. It's all kinds of dopeness.

Self-Care and a Culture of Running: Billy Mills as Role Model

Navajo children are taught to wake up and run to the east. As they begin their run, they let out a yell to celebrate the coming of a new day and be blessed by the gods. East is a significant direction in the Navajo culture, as it is the beginning of the lifecycle (Robinson & Muir, 2021). Running is woven into Navajo culture. It is seen as an important skill for the times when individuals are tested physically, emotionally, and spiritually. Running is seen as a healing process that will teach many lessons (Robinson & Muir, 2021).

Running is central in both the male and female puberty ceremonies. Kinaaldá is specifically a rite-of-passage ceremony that reinforces the feminine side of women. It is not the only identity-shaping event in the life of young Navajo women, but it is an important one relative to social and ethnic identity. Kinaaldá takes place over four days and occurs during a girl's first or second menstrual cycle, when it is thought that her powers are greatest. During those days, the young women have female mentors and teachers. They are taught how to work hard and how to take care of their mind, body, and spirit (Markstrom & Iborra, 2003).

Each day during Kinaaldá, young women must run two or three times, depending on local customs. The purpose of that running is to teach young women to take care of their bodies, to keep their bodies and immune systems strong and physically prepare for whatever they might go through. The length of the run is believed to predict the quality and longevity of each young woman's life (Markstrom & Iborra, 2003).

Historically, outside of ceremonies and spiritual connections, running was a central part of Indigenous communication and survival. Indigenous runners saved lives in many ways. Runners ran from house to house and village to village to spread news. In the high desert, runners kept watch for spring floods, alerting villagers and sprinting to the fields to capture water for that year's crops.

Many people run for physical health, but for Indigenous people, running is an act of survival connecting back to their culture and a tool used to maintain spiritual health. "I ran and then I felt spirituality. I could feel my feet pounding against the earth. I could breathe in, and if the wind [was] blowing in the right direction, a quarter of a mile away you'd see some wildflowers and I could inhale the fragrance of the flowers and it felt spiritual" (Tippett, 2016, transcript, para. 5). These are the words of Billy Mills, an Oglala Lakota distance runner who is best known for being the only U.S. Olympian to bring home the gold medal in the 10K. His performance at the 1964 Tokyo Olympics 10K final is considered one of the greatest comeback moments in sports history.

Mills, whose mother and father had both died by the time he was 12 years old, came into running as a source of healing. His running skills brought him to the University of Kansas in the late 1950s, but his experiences did not aid in continuing his healing. As he recalls:

> Society was breaking me. I was caught between Plessy vs. Ferguson, white and black America, equal but separate, being overturned with Brown vs. Board of Education. So, in many ways, if you were not a white athlete or a black athlete, you didn't fit into this change that was occurring in America, white leadership, black leadership, in conflict for equality. So, if you were maybe Latino, Hispanic, Native American, Asian, male, female, you didn't really fit into that equation, so I felt like I didn't belong, yet I was facing some of the racism. (Tippett, 2016, transcript, para. 9–10)

Mills recounted one specific racist experience in Kansas that pushed him close to suicide:

> When I made All-American, and this has happened on several occasions, many people were taking photographs, but there was always one photographer three years in a row who asked me to get out of the photo. And I remember a little bit of me breaking. I go back to my

hotel room and I'm going to jump. And I didn't hear it through my ears, I heard it underneath my skin. Movement. And the movement, in many ways, formed a word, the energy of the movement. I felt I could hear "Don't" four times. The fourth time powerful, gentle, loving, "Don't." And, to me, it was my dad's voice. (Tippett, 2016, transcript, para. 10–11)

This experience stopped Mills from taking his life and propelled him to write down his dream of winning a gold medal at the 1964 Olympics. He took the Indigenous traditions and spirituality and made them central to his Olympic training.

"I know what it is to be broken," Mills said, "but I also know what it is to be on a healing journey. You feel you're never healed, but the journey, you know, is a lifetime" (Tippett, 2016, transcript, para. 13).

Competency 3: Practice Love and Rage

My children have completely changed my connections to my emotions. Before I had children, I could have been described as "cold." Nothing bothered me more than seeing an adult cry. I didn't get it. Now I have a daughter and a son who are fully emotional beings. I believe I'm raising two empaths. Not only do they freely express their own emotions, but their ability to also tap into unspoken emotions of others is beautiful as well as jarring at the same time. Their expressions of feelings have pushed me to stay in that space of sadness, fear, frustration, and panic for much longer than I previously was comfortable with. They also have forced me not to label emotions as "good" or "bad." When they were young, the emotion often changed so quickly that I couldn't label it fast enough to respond, so I responded to whatever was in front of me, attached to this human that I loved, and I wanted to support and validate what they were feeling.

This experience as a mother has transferred to my interactions with others. I now ask others "How do you feel?" and "How did that comment/interaction land on you?" Giving space for others to express their emotions in the workplace has unlocked my own ability to express emotions and see the power in all emotions.

Author and activist bell hooks believed in the power of love and wrote a three-part series on its possibility and power. She believed that love had been mocked and separated from the quest for liberation and was not part of the liberation agenda. She heard Black and brown children talk about not seeing, understanding, or embracing the power of love of self, others, and community; so she resurfaced where love has always been a part of the Black experience and expressed the need for it to be part of the future of the Black experience (hooks, 2000).

In the first book of the trilogy, *All About Love*, hooks defines love as "a combination of trust, commitment, care, respect, knowledge, and responsibility" (2000, p. 54). She explains that love was an essential part of the liberation theology of Martin Luther King Jr., June Jordan, Zora Neale Hurston, and others who proclaimed through their speeches, poems, and stories the importance of building self-love, healthy self-esteem, and loving communities.

hooks further defines love by using the term "love ethic," a concept first expressed in the essay, "Nihilism in Black America" in *Race Matters* by Cornel West (1994): "A love ethic has nothing to do with sentimental feelings or tribal connections . . . self-love and love of others are both modes towards increasing self-valuation and encouraging political resistance in one's community" (p. 19). In *Salvation: Black People and Love*, hooks (2001) goes on to explain what a love ethic looks like in practice: "We can create love wherever we are. Valuing ourselves rightly means we understand love to be the only foundation of being that will sustain us in both times of lack and times of plenty" (p. 70). A love ethic is foundational for belief in ourselves and our country. Although the outcome of a love ethic is a unified community, narrower examples include engaging in positive thinking, refusing mindless consumption, and critical thinking.

bell hooks also embraced rage. In *Killing Rage*, she notes that "the rage of the oppressed is never the same as the rage of the privileged" (hooks, 1995, p. 30). She also shares her own journey toward becoming unashamed of her rage and embracing it to develop critical consciousness and relates how when she confronted her rage, it "moved me to grow and change, I understood intimately that it had the potential not only to destroy but also to construct. Then and now I understand rage to be a necessary aspect of resistance struggle" (p. 16). For hooks, rage can "act as a catalyst inspiring courageous action" (p. 16) and create "a passion for freedom and justice that illuminates, heals, and makes redemptive struggle possible" (p. 20).

Many contemporary perspectives on the power of rage as a key to liberation derive from the words of Audre Lorde in her 1981 keynote presentation, "The Uses of Anger," at the National Women's Studies Association Conference. She describes the power of rage, specifically in women:

> Every woman has a well-stocked arsenal of anger potentially useful against those oppressions, personal and institutional, which brought that anger into being. Focused with precision it can become a powerful source of energy serving progress and change. And when I speak of change, I do not mean a simple switch of positions or a temporary lessening of tensions, nor the ability to smile or feel good. I am speaking of a basic and radical alteration in those assumptions underlining our lives. (Lorde, 2007, p. 127)

Like hooks and Lorde, author and feminist Brittney Cooper (2019) sees the opportunity in rage. She first warns of the limitations of individual acts of rage and how it can destroy: "But the collective, *orchestrated fury* of Black women can move the whole world. . . . There is something clarifying about Black women's rage, something essential about the way it drills down to the core truth" (pp. 168–169). She goes on to say:

> Rage can help us build things, too. The clarity that comes from rage should also tell us what kind of world we want to see, not just what kind of things we want to get rid of. . . . If your rage can do anything for you, I hope it can do for you what it has done for me—help us to build the world we want to see. (pp. 273–274)

Philosopher Myisha Cherry (2022) discusses rage as a tool in the fight against racial injustice. In an interview for *The New Yorker* titled

"A Philosopher's Defense of Anger" (Rosner, 2021), Cherry refers to Audre Lorde in defining what she calls "Lordean rage":

> Lordean rage is very much focused on what we can do to make things better. If it destroys anything, it's going to destroy the patriarchy; it's going to destroy racist structures. But it's not trying to defeat people, or humiliate people. It's very focused on transformation.

This rage described by Cherry is different than white rage. In *White Rage: The Unspoken Truth of Our Racial Divide*, author Carole Anderson (2016) describes white rage with these words:

> White rage is not about visible violence, but rather it works its way through the courts, the legislatures, and a range of government bureaucracies. It wreaks havoc subtly, almost imperceptibly. Too imperceptibly, certainly, for a nation consistently drawn to the spectacular—to what it can *see*. It's not the Klan. White rage doesn't have to wear sheets, burn crosses, or take to the streets. Working the halls of power, it can achieve its ends far more effectively, far more destructively. (p. 3)

The "angry Black woman" trope has followed me throughout my leadership journey. I first ran away from showing emotion but then later embraced it as a power to bring people together. As Lorde (2007) notes, "It is not the anger of other women that will destroy us but our refusals to stand still, to listen to its rhythms, to learn within it, to move beyond the manner of presentation to the substance, to tap that anger as an important source of empowerment" (p. 121).

How to Practice Love and Rage

Practicing love and rage within the workplace may feel like you are opening yourself up to be hurt; however, it is about tapping into emotion to lead to action versus just staying in the space of emotion feeling paralyzed.

Focus on Action

Many of the leaders I spoke with talked about leading with love and the power of love. After a few conversations, as I kept hearing the reference to love, I started asking leaders to define and describe what "leading with love" looks and sounds like for them.

For Marco, a principal in a medium-size charter network in California, love is a decision and a commitment. "It's not a feeling. It could feel good, but feelings come and go, and I think love is a commitment that is beyond this moment. So, commitment to student success, commitment to equity is what I consider love." He went on to explain that love doesn't always feel good, and sometimes something that may feel negative is positive. "It feels very uncomfortable. . . . I feel the shame, but I feel the shame because I engage in this hurtful practice that I now reflect on. And I realized I got to change. That's love."

Benny, a Latino equity officer for a large charter network in New York, agreed that *love* is an action verb. "Love looks like patience. It looks like acknowledging that everyone is on their own journey. It looks like being able to put people's feet to the fire but hold their hand simultaneously." He went on to say, "So I lead with love in a way that's not about sugarcoating or not about not holding folks accountable, but it's about being courageous, being bold, being risky."

Love as defined by Marco and Benny is about using your deep care for someone or something to move you to action. My love makes me unwavering. I have a deep love for making sure Black and brown children see school as a caring yet academically demanding environment. Every action comes from that love. Love of my children.

Redefine the Trope

In 1887, journalist and activist Ida B. Wells wrote an article, "Our Women," that stated that the constant degradation of Black women throughout the history of the United States was an act of white-dominant culture trying to deter the movement toward liberation. The angry Black woman trope is long-lasting. There are other tropes that portray our anger as "unleashed," "out of control," and "animalistic." However, we know better. Embracing as our own that which is used to be oppressive takes away its power.

TaraShaun, a Black principal in a large district in Illinois, has had her passion be mistaken as anger. She joins a long line of leaders from the time of Ida B. Wells to today who are actively showing that Black women are more than just angry or magical, while also embracing their anger as a catalyst for change. TaraShaun uses her anger to push to keep high expectations for her students. She believes her passion is vital to her leadership.

Competency 4: Practice Self-Care

The term *intergenerational trauma* refers to the ways in which trauma experienced by people in one generation affects their descendants' health and well-being (DeAngelis, 2019). It was first studied with Holocaust survivors and their children; however, it is seen within cultural and ethnic groups around the world. Indigenous people had their land, language, and traditions stripped away from them. African Americans were kidnapped from their homeland and enslaved for hundreds of years. Asian Americans were placed in internment camps and killed while earning meager wages by building train tracks across the United States, and Latines lost their language and land (DeAngelis, 2019).

Because of this history, as well as continued discrimination and lack of opportunity, countless numbers of ABILPOC people suffer from intergenerational trauma. If unrecognized and untreated, it may result in mental illness, substance-use disorders, and suicide. Earlier in this chapter we saw how this trauma almost led Olympic gold medalist Billy Mills to suicide.

In addition to intergenerational trauma, the systemic racism that has remained in place since the forementioned events has resulted in ongoing racial trauma and injustices to ABILPOC people in the forms of racial profiling, redlining, voter suppression, and overrepresentation in the criminal justice system. Enduring constant prejudice, discrimination, and bias takes a toll on one's mental health. ABILPOC leaders often take on a "superman" persona that leads to burnout. They are pulled in many different directions throughout their day, month, and school year.

Issues of inequity do not stop after the school bell rings. ABILPOC leaders feel the inequities, microaggressions, and other forms of oppression in their personal life as well. Self-care is a necessary competency to continue to engage in the day-to-day work for the duration.

But we ABILPOC leaders are more than our pain. Love, rage, and self-care together are foundational for us. In the words of bell hooks (2001),

> Making the choice to love can heal our wounded spirits and our body politic. It is the deepest revolution, the turning away from the world as we know it, towards the world we must make if we are to be one with the planet—one healing heart giving and sustaining life. Love is our hope and our salvation. (p. 225)

How to Practice Self-Care—Physically

Just as Indigenous people connect running to physical, spiritual, and emotional well-being, my self-care practice has accumulated to tap into these three areas as well. In the context of my father passing away from cancer, the birth of my son, a new job, and then a move across the country, running quickly became my primary physical self-care ritual. I prefer to run at the beginning of the day, often before sunrise. This time by myself, outside and in the dark, gives me the stillness I need to start my day. Although I may have music, a podcast, or an audiobook playing in my ears, my thoughts usually take over. Pushing myself to go faster and further helps me take notice of my breath and my body and center myself for the rest of the day.

The COVID-19 pandemic gave many of the leaders I interviewed the opportunity to try new types of physical activity that had been more difficult to do when they were traveling to multiple school campuses throughout the day. Many incorporated daily walks, cycling, and weight training into their practice.

Mariane in California hadn't previously focused on physical self-care but found it to be helpful. "I tried to do the meditating thing," she said. "That didn't work. I'm very religious, but I'm terrible at praying and getting up early and reading my Bible and doing all the things I'm supposed to do. I found that I can talk to God more if I do my run.

So I do my run; I talk to God. And that runner's high is actually as addictive as people talk to you about. It's my time and sets me right to deal with the challenges of the day."

Owen, a Black equity officer in a large charter network in New York, has combined physical activity with meditation. "I thoroughly enjoy physical activity [exercise and competitive sports] whenever I can fit in the time," he said. "Recently I've taken up both boxing and meditation. I've never been able to fully understand the benefits of quieting my mind until I tried it. Anxiety, blood pressure, diet, and mental focus on slowing down have been some of the benefits of my introduction to meditation."

The combination of body and mind is why *My Grandmother's Hands* by Resmaa Menakem (2017) has become popular among ABILPOC teachers and leaders. Equity officers Angela in Texas and Jessica in Massachusetts have created spaces for self-care for staff through healing circles and book clubs using the text. Both of them integrate many of the strategies discussed, including deep breathing and humming.

How to Practice Self-Care—Mentally

Opportunities to work on your mind and bring a sense of peace and stillness show up in many ways. Enjoying a moment of laughter, cooking family recipes, and spending time with family were examples that leaders mentioned as times when they felt they were able to be present and practice love.

Intentionality in self-care was present through all the leaders' experiences. Gilmara in Iowa explained:

> I have a happy file that I have had for 20 years, in different shapes some years, but I store everything positive I receive from anybody in that file. So if I am having a bad day, I open that file and I read those things. That is so important in this work, because it's so draining if you're doing it right. And if you're . . . dismantling things, it's not easy. It's emotionally and physically demanding. So it helps me reinforce my commitment to the work and to the impact that I'm making. That file has been extremely useful for me in terms of refilling my energy when I am low.

Another strategy Gilmara shared is to show gratitude. She described her specific approach:

> Every Friday I save an hour in my schedule to thank people that were important for me that week. I do think that that generates a cycle of gratitude that is restoring. And sometimes we don't thank people. I do think that thanking the people who pushed you the most or who challenged you the most or who supported you the most is super important.

Being conscious of time, calendars, and boundaries was another common practice. Danielle from Florida shared the importance of disconnecting:

> Especially when it comes to DEI [diversity, equity, and inclusion] work, this is a lot on your shoulders, especially when you can also be a victim to oppression and being marginalized. And so, I just learned to turn it off, unplug, the minute the work day is over, over the weekend. I've learned to not overexert myself, and I'm fortunate that I have a supervisor that believes in that as well.

Similarly, the equity officers in Iowa and central Texas set personal boundaries for themselves. For Gilmara in Iowa, this means taking time after individual coaching sessions to breathe and transcribe notes, as well as canceling meetings when the calendar gets overwhelming. When Angela in central Texas receives an email asking her to join a committee or attend a meeting, she asks about the purpose and intended outcomes and how many meetings are required.

Patty, a Black equity officer in a medium-size district in California, explained her approach this way: "Not allowing someone to put me in a corner, whether it's a comment, whatever it is, making sure to address that, because then otherwise, you're constantly thinking about it."

Many leaders mentioned therapy as a necessary part of their mental self-care, as well as journaling. Although I often feel like running serves many purposes for me and makes me a better person, I have learned that it doesn't always provide everything I need. I used to need only a few minutes to fall into a deep sleep at night. Unfortunately, the COVID-19 pandemic, coupled with the national racial reckoning, affected my sleep patterns. I would lay awake at night just looking at the ceiling, hoping to fall asleep as my mind raced. The connection that I had gotten from my run at the beginning of the day faded by bedtime. So I began to journal, committing to writing one page a night—whatever comes to my mind. In looking back through the pages, the content is often a chronical of my run, my writing, and my reading. However, I do have memories and dreams that I make sure to put down on paper.

No matter what the action, the words of Laurice in Wisconsin are worth noting: "I think just finding joy and pleasure and the things that I want to do and with no apologies certainly is self-care." As her observation suggests, the effort does not always have to be about struggling; it can be about thriving.

How to Practice Self-Care—Spiritually

As noted earlier, Indigenous communities see running as a spiritual practice. Shaun Martin is the athletic director at Chinle High School in Arizona, an ultramarathoner, and the founder and race director of the Canyon de Chelly Ultramarathon. In an interview he did for the podcast *Running Realized*, he suggested that as runners head east in the morning, they yell out loud—as loudly as they can—to clear the passageway so "father sky can bring life into you." He goes on to explain how running can be a spiritual practice:

> Start to feel the earth with your feet. What do you want to tell the earth? What will the earth tell you? Start to think about your heartbeat. Align your footstep, heartbeat, and breath in unison—this is a way to tap into the energy of the holy people. Then pray. As you head home, think about the day being good and reflect on your run. (Robinson & Muir, 2021)

In my conversations with ABILPOC leaders, I found that their spiritual practices included connection with a higher power as well as with others. A daily ritual was important for spiritual practice. Tauheedah, a Black equity officer in a large district in Georgia, shared how she came to value rituals:

> Every morning I start [with] just being grateful for having the oppor-tunity to exercise what I feel is God's grace—my purpose and my faith in action in my profession. Then when I come home, I meditate, I do yoga; that's my routine to decompress and is part of my sanctuary. Then I'm grounded in my faith and my beliefs.

Similarly, Monica in Florida explained her ritual: "I start my day with prayer, meditation, and reading scripture and devotionals."

An affirming community is also part of spiritual practice. Jessica, a black equity officer in a small district in Massachusetts, stays con-nected to things that affirm her identity. She is active in the local chapter of her sorority and the alumni association from her alma mater. Sim-ilarly, Stephen, a Vietnamese American equity officer in California, shared the benefits of community:

> Being in community and charging, recharging with folks who I feel like I can connect with and don't have to code-switch . . . it's such a luxury when I'm able to be in a community of all Asians who come from the same experience or similar experiences.

In *The Fire Next Time*, James Baldwin (1963a) says, "Love takes off the masks that we fear we cannot live without and know we cannot live within" (p. 95). The last piece of my personal self-care puzzle is connection. Connection to those who love me as I am gives me the opportunity to take off Baldwin's mask and the mask of Paul Laurence Dunbar in his poem "We Wear the Mask." I have committed to con-nections to others—old friends that I haven't seen in years, as well as new ones who are experiencing a similar journey. Love of self, love of family, love of community, love of land, love of culture—these are all pieces of self-preservation.

Conclusion

I learned at a young age the rage that results from being judged or minimized simply because of my race. I was only 5 years old, and I was angry. I used that anger to prove my teacher wrong. I would continue to feel the "killing rage" described by bell hooks almost every year in my K–12 education and on into my leadership journey. Sometimes the rage manifests itself in tears. Love has been the only emotion that can match my rage.

Although professional standards may say that emotions should not be a part of the workplace, emotions *are* the workplace. To show up for yourself and the students and communities you serve requires being conscious of your own emotions and giving yourself the space to take care of yourself. It is the way to lead.

Key Takeaways

- Love and rage are revolutionary acts that bring communities together. Recognizing these emotions in yourself and tapping into them in others can connect communities on a deeper, more intimate level.
- Love and rage are intricately connected and are necessary for ABILPOC leaders who are working toward liberation. There are no such things as "bad" emotions, just bad actions because of emotions.
- Self-care can be experienced individually and in community. How you maintain or regain your energy is not as important as long as it happens and is part of your regular routine.
- Self-care can include physical, mental, and spiritual components. Recognizing that your body needs to be filled in more than one way can bring a centering of yourself that is more powerful than exercise or therapy alone.
- Self-care can occur in many forms and practices. A trial period may lead you to conclude that you cannot make certain practices a habit. Keep trying, however, knowing that your personal self-care practice will not look the same as those of friends or family members.

"Taking It Further" Reflection Questions

- How does intergenerational trauma show up for you, and how are you responding to its impact?

- Take an inventory of moments, experiences, and interactions that make you feel good and bring you joy. How can these help you start a self-care practice?
- Reflect on your current self-care practice. Is it feeding you physically, spiritually, and mentally?
- Are you suppressing or embracing your rage? How? Why? How can you embrace more?
- How can you show more love toward yourself and others?

Additional Resources

- In *Love and Rage: The Path of Liberation Through Anger*, Lama Rod Owens (2020) teaches how to harness the power of rage as a path toward spiritual and social change.
- In *Whistling Vivaldi: How Stereotypes Affect Us and What We Can Do*, Claude M. Steele (2010) combines his own personal experiences with his research on stereotype threats and identity.
- In *The Peace Chronicles*, each poem in this collection celebrates the freedom that brings author Yolanda Sealey-Ruiz (2021) tranquility, contentment, and joy.
- In the TEDx talk "Finding Home Through Poetry," poet and author Najwa Zebian (2016) shares how she discovered writing and speech as a way to find her place in new communities and countries.
- The National Day of Racial Healing occurs every year on the Tuesday following Martin Luther King Jr. Day. The purpose of the day is to directly name the systemic racism and harm experienced by minoritized communities and build trust and community to create a more just society.

5

Saying It and Naming It

When I dare to be powerful—to use my strength in the service of
my vision, then it becomes less and less important whether I am
afraid.

—Audre Lorde

"I lead with love in a way that's not about sugarcoating or not about holding folks accountable, but it's about being courageous, being bold, being
risky," says Benny Vazquez. He assumed the position of chief equity officer at the KIPP Foundation after leading his own nonprofit organization,
Crossing Borders, for many years. He has been working with leaders within
the organization to see the connections across identities, content areas,
and experiences. In conversations and actions, he has been successful
because of his ability to "say it and name it" with love.

Naming intersectional identities for himself and others has been a critical conversation point. As he explains:

One of the things that I like to think about is that we can't look at different identities without looking at it through the lens of race in this country and white supremacy. And so, when I think of intersectionality, it's not like I'm thinking about sexuality here and then religion over there, but I'm looking at it through [the question] "What does it mean for me to be a queer man of color in opposition to a white queer man?" Like we have different experiences, even though we share the same marginalized identity.

He has also had to name anti-blackness, which shows up with folks wanting to focus on socioeconomic class versus race, or Latine colleagues not seeing themselves in the conversation about race. He has heard folks say, "What are you talking about? Like, I'm not that." However, he has named the connections that are hindering progress:

Someone who's Latinx doesn't understand that the more that we fight for Black liberation, including those Latinos who are Black, that liberation also includes social-economic liberation. And so, there's no way that we could talk about social-economic class without talking about race. Capitalism is grounded and was formed on the backs of enslaved Africans. So if you want to talk about socioeconomic class, let's start there. And so that further division is what causes there to be so much tension sometimes around this organizing work between Latinx and Black folks. And let's start with the fact that social-economic class is also a pathway to citizenship status. It's a pathway to immigration policy. And a lot of immigration policies are anti-brown and anti-black. And so we can't separate the two. If we separate the two, we are supporting white supremacy in a way that gets us to not talk about blackness.

Naming the separation between academics and equity has also been a charge for Benny. Here's how he describes it:

[Some think] that the academic success of our kids is on one side of the aisle and that equity work is on the other side of the aisle. However, if you have a school that's grounded in treating kids with humanity and love and respect, kids will have an increased joy in learning. Therefore, teachers will be happier and therefore, academics will increase, economic success will *increase. We can't separate academic success and equity, because they're together. They are intrinsically merged.*

Benny also makes the point in conversations. "*I tend to interrupt, but I'm not in the business of calling people out unless they are admittedly being racist,*" he says. If he hears a phrase or comment that needs to be addressed, he might say, "*My request for you is to think about what you just said and why. You don't have to do it right now, but I ask that you reflect on it. We can reflect on it together if you want, but you need to know that what you said landed difficult for me.*"

All the instances of saying it and naming it are done with love, patience, and vulnerability. Recall the quote from Benny in Chapter 4 about leading with love: "*[Leading with] love looks like patience. It looks like acknowledging that everyone is on their own journey. It looks like being able to put people's feet to the fire but hold their hand simultaneously.*" He elaborates:

[It's about being able] to ensure that you're seeing the best possible representation of that person in your eyes, even when they don't show up that way. It's grounding conversations in a way that challenges, but also acknowledges the humanity that you are coming into this with.

Benny provides this final point of reflection: "*If I am able to model vulnerability in ways that can actually move your organization forward, it can serve as an example as to how others can also have the permission, especially folks of color, . . . to be vulnerable.*"

Crossing Borders: Yuri Kochiyama as Role Model

On December 7, 1941, Mary Yuriko Nakahara's life changed forever. She had just returned home from teaching Sunday school in San Pedro, California, when there was a knock on the door. Three FBI agents wanted to see her father. Within minutes, the agents woke her sleeping father, who was recovering from ulcer surgery, and took him away. Earlier that day, Pearl Harbor had been attacked by Japanese bombers. The next day, the agents came back and searched the entire house. For days the family didn't know where their father was. Eventually he returned home, seriously ill; he passed away a day later (Hung, 2002).

Soon after her father's death, Yuri, age 20, and her mother and brothers were sent to an internment camp in Jerome, Arkansas, where they spent two years. Yuri kept busy by writing letters to Nisei soldiers, including her twin brother, and welcoming new arrivals at the camp's entrance with music. Her time spent in the all-Japanese environment cultivated her racial pride (Fujino, 2009).

Yuri's pride turned toward activism when she married Bill Kochiyama, a decorated veteran of the Japanese American 442nd Regimental Combat Team of the U.S. Army. The couple became involved in community activities in New York City, including opening their tiny apartment to social gatherings for Japanese American and Chinese American soldiers headed for service in the Korean War.

In the early 1960s, Yuri, Bill, and their six kids moved to a new housing development in Harlem. They enrolled in the Harlem "freedom schools" to learn about Black history and culture. Soon Yuri began participating in sit-ins such as the one at the Downstate Medical Center in Brooklyn to demand jobs for Black people and Puerto Ricans, and inviting Freedom Riders to speak at weekly open houses in the family's apartment (Fujino, 2009).

As a middle-aged Japanese American woman, Yuri earned her respect slowly in Black groups. She eventually dropped her first name, Mary, in favor of her middle one. "In the '60s everyone was changing their names," she said. "I was in a couple of black groups and my daughter said, 'Mom, you can't go in there as Mary'" (Hung, 2002, para. 57). It was also during this time that Yuri met Malcolm X. She was Malcolm X's pen pal during his trip to Africa, receiving his postcards from nine different countries, and was by his side when he was murdered.

Yuri's ties to the civil rights movement of the mid-20th century made her a leader of the Asian American movement that emerged in the late 1960s and sought to unite Asian Americans in social, political, and other types of activism. In New York City, she joined Asian Americans for Action, which provided a platform for her denunciation of U.S. imperialism in Vietnam, Okinawa, and elsewhere; advocacy for the teaching of ethnic studies at the City College of New York; and support for the hiring of Chinese construction workers at Confucius Plaza, a housing complex in Chinatown (Fujino, 2009). She was a strong voice in the campaign for reparations and a formal government apology for Japanese American internees. The 1988 Civil Liberties Act signed by President Ronald Reagan provided an apology and $20,000 to each surviving internee. Nearly half of the internees had already died by then (Fujino, 2009).

In addition to bridging the Black and Asian civil rights movements, Yuri became a supporter of the Young Lords, a Chicago-based organization that advocated on behalf of Puerto Rico and various Latine populations. In 1977, she was one of 30 people who stormed the Statue of Liberty and held it for nine hours to bring attention to the struggle for Puerto Rican independence (Hung, 2002). Yuri was a constant critic of the United States government and continued to "name and say," including pointing out the similarities between her internment and the detainment and harassment of thousands of Middle Easterners following the 9/11 attacks (Hung, 2002). Summarizing Yuri's approach to life, Hung (2002) says:

> To be a Movement person is to live a life of losses, yet still retain hope. And Yuri never lets go of hope. She may forget things now, but she learns them again. When, in rare moments, she has time to herself, she takes Malcolm's edict to "know history" at heart, and devours history books. (para. 100)

Competency 5: Engage in Authentic Dialogue

Conversations are one of the primary vehicles used by leaders of color to engage individuals who may vary in their understanding, willingness, and commitment to creating an equitable school system. In seeking to make these conversations authentic and impactful, you, as an ABILPOC leader, must recognize the vulnerability, historical distrust, and risk involved when talking about identity in terms of knowing and recognizing both your past, present, and future as well as that of the person you are conversing with.

In *Race Talk and the Conspiracy of Silence: Understanding and Facilitating Difficult Dialogues on Race*, author Derald Wing Sue explains that for many people, having conversations about race was not part of their upbringing. When I discuss this observation with others, I talk about the fact that race *was* a topic of conversation for me at our dining room table. On the one hand, I was raised in a traditional Baptist household where, as I mentioned before, we sang, "Red and yellow, black or white, we are precious in His sight," and color blindness was heralded in church; but on the other hand, my brothers and sisters and I were being raised in the most segregated city in the country at the time. The topic of how we were going to be perceived as Black kids in Milwaukee, Wisconsin, was always discussed. In conversations about identity, particularly across differences, it is often the lack of knowledge, history, and perspective that makes the conversation difficult.

In Chapter 3, we talked about the cycle of socialization and its impact. Here, too, socialization plays into our abilities to have conversations about identity. Research by Apfelbaum and his colleagues (2008) suggests the following:

> [A]t some point after mastering categorization and generalization across classes of stimuli, children [at 10 years of age] learn that by applying these same principles to people—describing others on the basis of skin color—they risk appearing prejudiced and might receive social sanctions. (p. 1516)

The researchers go on to explain:

> Some suggest that this decline reflects a genuine decrease in prejudice resulting from increased perspective taking during the acquisition of concrete operations, yet others suggest it represents an increasing desire to adhere to societal norms and engage in self-presentation. (p. 1517)

Socialization also encourages us to gather. In author Priya Parker's 2019 TED Talk, "3 Steps to Turn Everyday Get-Togethers into Transformative Gatherings," she presents ways to reinvent gatherings so they are more enjoyable and meaningful for everyone. Her first step is to ensure there is a specific, indisputable purpose for bringing people together. The second step is to cause "good controversy." She explains further that to generate good healthy controversy, the environment needs to be created. There needs to be some element of trust in order for conflict to be embraced. The final step in creating a meaningful gathering is to create a temporary alternative world with what she calls "pop-up rules." Parker admits that this may sound controlling, but when you are gathering people across differences, unspoken norms could become detrimental. Instead, being clear and specific constructs a temporary space to connect and make meaning together.

Many people describe conversations about identity as "difficult." Verta Maloney, a multitalented, ground-breaking, beautiful-inside-and-out friend of mine, introduced me to the phrase "unpracticed conversations," which I quickly embraced. Like learning anything else, learning how to have conversations about identity becomes easier once you have them numerous times, with as many people as possible.

How to Engage in Authentic Dialogue

Practicing may not be effective when it lacks guidance and structure. Some ways to practice engaging in authentic dialogue are agreeing to disagree, seeing the whole person, educating, asking questions, sharing your experiences, and using a framework.

Agree to Disagree

The purpose and result of authentic dialogue may not be agreement. Instead, it may be to learn how to disagree and be inclusive at the same time. Gilmara, an equity officer in Iowa, shared her experience with staff after organizing speakers to discuss the rights of the LGBTQIA+ community:

> We went through with the program. We did it, and I told them, . . . listen, members of the LGBTQ community are in our buildings, they are in our schools, and regardless of your religious orientation, you've got to

embrace them. Even if you disagree with their choice or their sexual choices, you've got to include them.

She went on to remark that the conversation ended with her saying, "I'm not here to change your mind or your political or religious views. What I'm here to do is to help you include even when that clashes with your political and religious beliefs."

See the Whole Person

For equity officer Tauheedah in Georgia, seeing and valuing the humanity of people has been critical. She explained:

When you see and value the humanity of people, besides all the facade of the rhetoric that you hear, you actually learn a lot about folks and have a deeper appreciation for the humanity of folks. And . . . for me that's the second greatest lesson that I learned being in this role in the South, in particular. . . . I also want to name that that fear is a fear [of] the unknown. And it's coming from a fear of equity as a zero-sum game.

She shared that this approach has resulted in people who previously were naysayers becoming more receptive, because many people in her district feel that equity is race baiting. So she names everything upfront.

Educate

Sometimes dialogue must include education. Equity officer Mariane in California shared her approach:

Number one is education. I try to just pepper people with as much educational content as I can. It's programmed in me that when the lesson is needed, the teacher appears. I'm hoping that, as you pepper people with the educational content, when it comes to, "Oh, I have this question," I'm hoping that they know that the resources are there.

For Monica in Florida, her approach to education involves being direct. "My husband says I'm a natural-born confronter," she said. "So, for me it is being prepared with clear facts and information and not being afraid to speak. I would rather speak up than not." Tauheedah from Georgia also embraces opportunities for education:

> Every time is a teachable moment. Your approach can either put the person off and then you don't go anywhere and address the issue, or it can bring the person along to where you're trying to go and where you need them to go, because what they're talking about is going to have an adverse impact on kids.

Ask Questions

Another strategy is questioning. Mariane in California said, "I ask a lot of questions." Tauheedah in Georgia shared her specific approach: "One way in which I respond is I first ask clarifying questions—'Help me understand when you say X, Y, and Z,' or 'Why are you saying X, Y, and Z?' I genuinely want to know where that comment comes from." Gilmara in Iowa also leverages questioning: "If I am in a meeting and somebody says something that rubs me the wrong way, or that sounds inappropriate or not inclusive, instead of making a judgment and telling them, 'This was racist,' I'll say, 'What you said stopped me in my tracks and caused me to stop and reflect. Can you clarify that for me?'"

Share Your Experiences

Tauheedah from Georgia uses her personal experience to connect with others. She explained:

> I found that a lot of their experiences are similar to my experience, and a lot of the ways in which they view the world aren't that different from the way I view the world, or that may be just different in terms of their racial lens that they're adding to it, and my racial lens that I'm adding to it.

Mariane in California also leverages her personal experience to engage people. Here's how she described her approach:

> Sometimes I even throw myself in the fire a little bit, where I'll say, "Well, in my experience, I know this is something that I've done. And being a person of color or being an immigrant to this country, being

a person who has experienced discrimination and bigotry, if I can say that I have done things that I'm not proud of, I hope you can too."

David, a Black equity officer in a large district in Maryland, explained that being more intentional in sharing multiple parts of his identity has proved to be important:

I must be more explicit so that people can see the fullness of what's behind me as I invite them to do the same things for themselves—in terms of socioeconomic background and how I grew up, where I come from, educational things that I've experienced, injustices I've experienced, injustices that I've dished out. Those are the kinds of things I must state for people so that, again, they can do the same for themselves. But I have to show the complexity of who I am, because that exists in all of us.

Use a Framework

Finally, developing a framework for conversation may be helpful. Glenn Singleton's (2005) *Courageous Conversations About Race* introduces the four agreements as group norms, six conditions for participants to embody and practice, and the compass as a tool for participants to check in with their emotions. These tools together encourage, sustain, and deepen interracial dialogue about race. In Georgia, Tauheedah developed the equity communications framework called "DNA":

We start with *D*, [which] stands for *define*. So we define, make sure we're consistently using the same definitions for the common term. If we're saying "equity," we're using it the right way; if we're saying "social justice," we're saying, and we keep saying, this is the definition of equity. Then the *N* stands for *narrate*. We always make sure we take time to narrate our "why" for this work, that we share our data behind our "why" for this work. And then the *A* in DNA stands for another acronym [from] the Government Alliance for Racial Equity: *ACT* (Affirm, Counter, Transform). In your communications you must arm your shared core values to counter resistance and transform hearts and minds.

No matter what strategy these equity officers use, issues of inequitable language and practices must be addressed.

Competency 6: Attend to Relationships

Attending to relationships includes embracing coconspirators across race and culture. Moving toward others who don't have the same identity markers as you do will widen your perspective and provide you with stronger skills to support minoritized students and community members in your school system.

Engaging in authentic dialogue can be challenging. Equally challenging is building relationships across difference. Cross-difference friendships sometimes require one half of the relationship—usually the half with the minoritized characteristic—to leave a part of themselves out of the relationship for it to work and thrive. So why bother? In order for us to build an equitable school system, change needs to take place from all perspectives and sources of power. Tapping into that space requires tapping into difference.

Jean Baker Miller's 2008 paper "Connections, Disconnections, and Violations" explains that people develop by interaction with other people. No one develops in isolation. In these interactions, if people are not acting in ways that foster others' development, they inevitably are doing the reverse—that is, participating in interactions in ways that do *not* further other people's development. According to Miller, when a relationship is growth-producing, five things happen as a result: increased zest, a sense of empowerment, greater knowledge, an increased sense of self-worth, and a desire for more connection. Growth-producing relationships across difference can be impactful for incremental and long-term change.

In her book *Can We Talk About Race? And Other Conversations in an Era of School Resegregation,* Beverly Daniel Tatum (2008) describes a cross-racial friendship she has had for decades. Tatum, who is Black, notes that this friendship with a white colleague was somewhat unique, in that it emerged from work-related conversations about their individual experiences with race. She notes that the white friend had done intentional work on her "whiteness" and what it means to be white in a race-conscious society. In her book *Killing Rage*, bell hooks (1995) also gives advice on cross-racial relationships between women. She agrees with Tatum that when individual white women are equally aware of the history of racism in the United States and institutional efforts to keep the two groups apart, there is opportunity for deeper connection.

In Tatum's friendship, she and her colleague came together not as teacher and learner. Tatum didn't feel like she had to teach her friend anything about race. In her book, hooks speaks about how, in society, Black and white women are not positioned as equal. White women are positioned to be served and Black women to be the server. The two people in the relationship need to consciously commit to connect in their friendship on an equal level, breaking from societal norms.

Tatum (2008) ends her narrative by giving the reader three lessons for a flourishing cross-racial friendship. The first lesson is that "human connection requires familiarity and contact" (p. 100). There needs to be an effort to know the community. A second lesson is to be thoughtful about structure. "White people and people of color often come to the challenge of cross-racial connection with very different perspectives" (p. 101). White people prefer connection in a social environment, but ABILPOC individuals see social environments as breeding grounds for microaggressions and prefer structured environments. Tatum's final lesson is that "connection depends on frankness, and a willingness to talk openly about issues of race" (p. 102). In her final words of advice for Black and white women who want to create bonds, hooks (1995) says, "Such bonding is possible only if the two groups are willing to undergo processes of education for critical consciousness that support changes in thinking and behavior" (pp. 222–223).

In successful cross-cultural relationships, the intention and purpose must be grounded in working together to dismantle patriarchy, having accountability in each other, and showing a willingness to engage in self-interrogation.

How to Attend to Relationships

When I speak to anyone in a leadership role about their approach to their work, the importance of relationships is typically part of the conversation, especially if the person is new. The nuances of attending to these relationships isn't always explicitly talked about. Attending to relationships involves the following behaviors: showing humanity and humility, setting explicit intentions, and choosing wisely.

Show Humanity and Humility

Gilmara in Iowa explained why, for her, humility is essential to building relationships:

> The first thing I think is to show up with humility. I always say to people, I don't know everything, and I want to keep learning, and I recognize I am a work in progress. So that's the first thing, because I think when you set the tone of humility, the other person displays humility too. It's not a power struggle of who knows more.

Tauheedah in Georgia also spoke about humanity as a critical factor:

> I humanize myself. I'm more than my skin color. So I share my stories. I come in the room, and I start with relationships. So before we talk about any difficult inequitable issue, [I'll say,] "How are you? Who are you? Tell me more about you. Tell me about your family." So I start every conversation with sharing me. I claim my humanity, and I feel like that's important in this work—to claim your humanity and your dignity.

Set Explicit Intentions

Another shared strategy is to be explicit in your intentions for the relationship. "I always express my intention from the get-go and explicitly," explained Gilmara. She continued:

> Because a lot of times our intentions are very similar, but our approaches are very different. So using our intention as a bridge helps you connect with the person and decide on the best approach that it could land so that the decision is meaningful. And so, I always express my intention in a very clear and explicit way.

When I am forging relationships, this approach may sound like me asking the person, "What do you want us to learn from each other?"

or "What are some questions that we both have that we could help each other answer?" These questions help establish equality in the relationship, as well as give it purpose.

Choose Wisely

A final recommendation is to be intentional regarding who you are building relations with and why. Monica in Florida related that within two weeks on the job she met with more than 100 people via Zoom. She went on to say:

> That meeting started these spin-off connections, and then this person introducing me to this person. And I think you just need to be really sincere. You need to be a really good listener. People need to know that you understand their challenges, or you recognize the challenges, and you're going to do everything you can to make things right. But also, understanding the way to do this is by fixing the system and that it's not just one person's job to undo.

Gilmara, the Iowa equity officer, shared her goal for challenging conversations: "I have had several difficult conversations. . . . My measurement is, I need to leave this room closer to this person than [when] I entered."

Conclusion

I start almost all my presentations, trainings, and speeches by telling the story of myself and the "why" behind the work that I do. Sharing the story of my upbringing and the challenge of raising a Black daughter and son sets the stage for listening and connecting. Interacting across difference is challenging, especially when the topic can lead to misunderstanding, hurt, or pain. Societal circumstances and pressures don't help either. Combining storytelling and deep listening can create the support that is necessary. Storytelling improves listening skills. Storytelling that includes other strategies that educate and show vulnerability can also lead to stronger and more productive conversations.

Key Takeaways

- Having unpracticed conversations about identity must come with a set of strategies to ensure you meet the intended outcomes. Not all strategies will work for you, but don't be afraid to try several and adapt depending on the direction the conversation is taking.
- Showing your own vulnerability and humanity is important to talk and build relationships across difference. This effort is not about exploiting your story but about being transparent with what brought you to engage in and continue in the conversation.
- Whatever strategy you use, the important part is to say something and leave the conversation with a better understanding of each other.

"Taking It Further" Reflection Questions

- Reflect on the last conversation you had. Which strategies could you have used to generate a better outcome for everyone involved?
- Considering the value of engaging in conversation, who is the person or persons who would be most helpful in widening your lens to experiences you need to learn more about?
- Reflect on the last time a decision was made or a comment was said that you didn't respond to. What held you back? What do you need to do so that the next time that situation occurs you will say something?

Additional Resources

- In *Some of My Best Friends: Writings on Interracial Friendships*, editor Emily Bernard (2004) asked a group of writers to respond, based on their experiences, to questions about interracial friendships.
- In *So You Want to Talk About Race,* author Ijeoma Oluo (2018) addresses the challenges of engaging in, and offers concrete strategies for, authentic dialogue about race.

- In *The Art of Gathering*, Priya Parker (2018) gives concrete advice on how to make coming together more meaningful and productive.
- In *Why Are All the Black Kids Sitting Together in the Cafeteria? And Other Conversations About Race*, Beverly Daniel Tatum (1997), a renowned authority on the psychology of racism, argues that straight talk about our racial identities is essential if we are serious about communicating across racial and ethnic divides and pursuing antiracism.

6

Building Coalitions

Without community, there is no liberation.

—Audre Lorde

"I value partnerships and coconspirators; I seek out natural connections, and they often find me because of the way I do my work with love; so people come and find me because they want to be connected to the work because they find it fulfilling as well."

Angela Ward's career includes more than 12 years serving in equity-related positions in the Austin Independent School District in Texas. She has been leading for equity since before it became a common term in mission statements and strategic plans and before the widespread hiring of diversity officers.

A self-described Southern girl from Houston, Angela grew up in an unapologetic Black household. It was this upbringing that showed her the *inequities faced by her family, community, and others who looked like her. Her experiences led her to pursue degrees in criminal justice and educational administration and eventually receiving her doctoral degree focused in cultural studies at the University of Texas at Austin.*

While serving in the Austin ISD, Angela's love-focused approach gave her space to work with new teachers and principals as well as create a two-year cohort program in which staff members learned about cultural proficiency and then became trainers of others. Angela's coconspirators advocated on her behalf to expand her staff, and her relationship building resulted in the Race Equity Council that included students, teachers, and community-based organizations.

Angela dreamed of starting a Student Equity Council as the district engaged deeper with students through the districtwide No Place for Hate effort. With assistance of the Race Equity Council, she supported equity-centered student agency work at various high schools. In 2018, she launched a Race Equity Leadership yearlong course at a high school and a semester course at a middle school. A few interested students enrolled. The curriculum was designed to support the development of an equitable understanding of their lived experiences as students and to develop their voice to create opportunities to support each other and their peers as they navigate issues important to them at school and in the school district. Their voices were loud and clear in the height of the global health crisis. The group of high school students consciously shared their perspectives, hurts, and harms and informed adults in the community and their schools of their needs.

The Race Equity Leadership course seeded the beginning of the districtwide Student Equity Council in December 2020. The students learned liberatory design and grappled with barriers to liberated schools. They learned to use the Courageous Conversations About Race Protocol to listen, hear, and share dialogue and learning space together.

Angela has faced, and continues to face, challenges as a Black woman leading within a white space. She leverages her knowledge of the history of public education in the United States and connects it with questions to understand what the root cause of the concern is. In one particular meeting that was focused on a systemic issue, a participant inserted a perspective focused on the behavior of the individual. Angela's response? "I do a lot of listening and don't take it personally. I listen to hear the complaint under the complaint. I pay attention to what I know about the system to provide some type of understanding as someone who is working to create identity-safe space." Angela's favorite question is "What are your intended outcomes?"

Angela believes that to be successful, leaders for equity need to use what they know about the system and be able to successfully navigate whiteness. They need to partner with those who are already doing the work in the system. There is work being done; they just need to find it. Her advice to school systems is to not require a leader for equity to be the lone voice. "They need to work hand in hand with the superintendent. They also need a budget, a staff, and be able to hire who they need to get the work done."

Collaborating in the Movement: Ella Baker as Role Model

Ella Baker believed that the most oppressed sectors of society had to be at the forefront of the struggle to change society, and that belief kept her focused on building coalitions. In every strategy session and meeting she participated in, everyday people were at the center of the conversation to change their community.

In 1952, Ella Baker was elected president of the New York City branch of the NAACP, becoming the first woman to hold that position. Although she represented the NAACP, this affiliation did not stop her from representing other organizations or forming coalitions with other groups across the city. During her time in the role, one of her major focuses was school reform (Ransby, 2003). She collaborated with noted scholars and educators such as Kenneth and Mamie Clark during the 1950s to desegregate schools and to usher in community-based, progressive approaches to education such as those her own niece was experiencing in the Quaker school she attended. Although the images one sees of the aftermath of the Brown v. Board of Education decision focus on integration, Baker and her allies went beyond this, calling for greater parent and community involvement in running the schools.

Baker took her coalition-building philosophy to the South and during her time there led the development of collaborations across race, class, and philosophies. She arrived just a few years after the murder of 14-year-old Emmett Till in 1955. While visiting his relatives in Mississippi, Till had gone to a store and been accused by the white store clerk of whistling at her. The woman's husband and brother-in-law kidnapped and brutally murdered Till, dumping his body in the Tallahatchie River. Till's mother's decision to have an open-casket funeral created the "Emmett Till Generation," a generation of young African Americans who joined the civil rights movement to demand equal treatment under the law (Library of Congress, n.d.).

In collaboration with Bayard Rustin and Stanley David Levison, Baker created the blueprint for the Southern Christian Leadership Conference (SCLC) in 1957. Many saw the SCLC as a rival to the NAACP. Others worried that the new organization would be affiliated with communists, hence the use of the word *Christian* in the name. Baker was not interested in grandstanding, and the male-dominated movement did not respond well to her directness and willingness to ask questions; but her experience and impact propelled her from serving as a volunteer to becoming interim executive director.

Baker had an ability to straddle organizational divides steeped in personal rivalries and ideological battles. In most Southern towns in the 1950s and 1960s, a class bias positioned middle- and upper-class Black people as the natural leaders and spokespersons for the race, to the exclusion of others. There were also two distinct approaches to activism: the tempered radicals, who bargained for incremental change, and the abolitionists, who were outspoken and wanted immediate change. Although the tempered radicals complained about the abolitionists' tactics, the two approaches were at times complementary (Ransby, 2003).

Additionally, Baker was a woman, and women generally didn't assume public-facing roles at the time. Within all these circumstances,

Baker managed nevertheless. The message she taught to the young organizers was simple and subtle: Listen to the oppressed communities and understand the ways they see and analyze the world. Check your own ego and personal ambitions to be in service to the communities in front of you (Ransby, 2003). This approach, along with her patience, tolerance, and willingness to work with individuals of diverse ideologies, helped her pull together locally based organizers across the South to advocate for initiatives.

Baker also worked across racial lines. She helped to forge an important biracial alliance between the African American and Puerto Rican communities. Baker also encouraged her younger organizers to look beyond the Black community and beyond the United States. She maintained international connections by building personal relationships with people from around the world who visited the United States, and she wanted the next generation to also take an interest in global politics and to travel and meet activists from other countries (Ransby, 2003).

In Baker's view, members of an effective coalition must learn and grow together. Her approach leveraged the individual skills of each member to focus on a collective goal. Her communal approach was duplicated by the women's movement of the 1970s, and she continued to use this approach later in her life to support the campaign to free the jailed activist Angela Davis and contribute to efforts to end apartheid in South Africa.

Baker's philosophy, which is embodied by organizers today, was that "oppressed people did not need a messiah to deliver them from oppression; all they needed was themselves, one another, and the will to persevere" (Ransby, 2003, p. 188).

Competency 7: Create a Coalition

Ubuntu. A South African word, it has no equivalent in English. Archbishop Desmond Tutu (1999) described it as follows:

> My humanity is caught up, is inextricably bound up, in yours. . . .
> A person with *ubuntu* is open and available to others, affirming of others, does not feel threatened that others are able and good, for

he or she has a proper self-assurance that comes from knowing that he or she belongs in a greater whole and is diminished when others are humiliated or diminished, when others are tortured or oppressed, or treated as if they were less than who they are. (p. 31)

Ngogi Mahaye is a member of the Executive Council of the Department of Education in the South African province of KwaZulu-Natal. He explains ubuntu as follows:

Ubuntu is simultaneously the foundation and the edifice of African philosophy. It is the basis of African communal cultural life, it functions as a unifying factor, bringing people together regardless of their background or access to wealth. One's humanity cannot be separated from the humanity of those around him. It is an individual existence of the self and the simultaneous existence for others. One becomes fully human to the extent that he/she is included in relationships with others. (Mahaye, 2018)

Although the word ubuntu cannot be translated into English, its attributes and characteristics can be felt in coalitions built ever since Ella Baker provided the blueprint. As the murder of Emmitt Till galvanized a generation in the mid-1950s, other incidents have since brought people to together to demand change for the better.

In 1971, the Third World Women's Alliance (TWWA) was created by the Liberation Committee of the Student Nonviolent Coordinating Committee (SNCC). The TWWA expanded the topics addressed earlier by women activists to include areas such as sterilization abuse, infant mortality, welfare rights, and low-wage work. The TWWA's focus on the "third world" brought the struggles of women in Latin America, Asia, Africa, and the Middle East to the front while also tackling the issues of racism and sexism in the United States (King, 1988).

After the killing of Trayvon Martin in 2012, Arab American, Black, and Latine youth marched from Daytona Beach to Sanford, Florida, and formed the Dream Defenders. Its "Freedom Papers" document is a call to action for a country "of safety and security—away from prisons, deportation, and war—and towards healthcare, housing, jobs, and movement for all" (Dream Defenders, n.d.).

The Carolina Federation describes itself as "a statewide organization that brings local people together across race and the rural-urban divide to build political and electoral power in their own communities and across North Carolina" (Carolina Federation, n.d.). A recent effort involved registering Black and Latine voters for the 2020 presidential election (Araiza, 2021).

In Chicago, the mission of a group called InterAction is "to activate and advance Young Black, Indigenous, People of Color and their counter-narratives to build a more just, inclusive, and equitable society" (InterAction, n.d.). They established the Young Black and Asian Solidarity Working Group to promote coalition building between the two communities (Araiza, 2021; InterAction, n.d.).

In 2021, as school boards and state legislatures were looking to ban books and eliminate the teaching of critical race theory (CRT) in K–12 schools, a new wave of coalitions was created, led by young people. In the Central York School District in Pennsylvania, the Panther Anti-Racist Union was created to organize protests to fight for more diversity in the curriculum and against censoring of books (Branigin, 2022). Similarly, the Georgia Youth Justice Coalition formed in 2021 to train young people in how to testify at state legislative hearings and school board meetings to stop gerrymandering of districts in the surrounding Atlanta area (Timm, 2021).

A strong and effective coalition can broaden your base of support and trust; enhance your potential to gain attention and effect change; provide talents, skills, and resources that can be shared to achieve program goals; and propel a strategic and concerted resolution of the problem. Coalitions thrive when each individual puts their own personal feelings and need for individualism aside and willingly comes together.

When everyone in the coalition shares responsibility, goals, decisions, and leadership and energetically and enthusiastically works toward a common goal, the coalition has the potential for great success. You may not need to build a formal coalition, but having someone in your corner is still essential. You cannot be on the path to dismantling systemic racism on your own.

In today's school systems, ABILPOC leaders need to note the characteristics and tactics used by Ella Baker and those who came after her to create their own internal and external coalitions. In *We Want to Do More Than Survive: Abolitionist Teaching and the Pursuit of Educational Freedom,* Bettina Love (2019) says, "We all thrive when everyday people resist, when everyday people find their voice, when everyday people demand schools that are students' homeplaces, and when everyday people understand that loving darkness is our path to humanity" (p. 68). ABILPOC leaders must actively seek out everyday people who are going to do the work alongside them.

How to Create a Coalition

The blueprint left by Ella Baker to create a coalition involves the following behaviors: having a clear objective, thinking beyond yourself, managing political landmines, adding layers, and creating more than one coalition.

Have a Clear Objective

As a leader, you will want to be concrete about the goals and outcomes of the coalition. In *Culturally Responsive School Leadership*, Muhammad Khalifa (2018) tells leaders that the objective should not just be focused on the school system but needs to be community-focused to engage the larger community in addressing it.

As an ABILPOC leader, your own intersectional identities will create assumptions about what your objectives are. You will have to move beyond assumptions to collectively develop an objective that is targeted yet inclusive. For example, because I am a Black woman, some may assume that I want to target Black girls in my initiatives. This is a valid assumption, given the data on how Black girls are targeted and punished within school systems. However, if I did decide to target Black girls, I would need to be clear that focusing on the minoritization of Black girls will highlight the minoritization of many other students, and the strategies we employ can be used across intersectional identities.

In Massachusetts, a large school district developed a racial equity planning tool to make its objectives clear. Henry, a Black man who recently served in the district's equity office, explained that the tool is used for all decisions, and the community expects that to be the case:

> We're going to go through a process to get to decisions, and we're going to be transparent about it . . . and we're going to do it to the letter of the document. And when you do that and people see you do it, they begin to trust you. I think we try to do what we say we're going to do.

The objective of the coalition you develop may be to identify the goals of the school system. The objective may be to serve as a support to you, provide a forum for discussion, create a ripple effect, or connect members within and outside the district. No matter the objective, you need to be able to know it and communicate it in a way that is understandable to the various community members you want to be part of your coalition.

Think Beyond Yourself

When thinking about the individuals in your coalition, the more diverse, nontraditional, and creative they are, the better the chances of the coalition succeeding. You will want to look for individuals who are credible, reputable members of the community. They should have strong links with the community and with decision makers. They also should be politically savvy or at least understand politics. Look around the table where you currently sit and think about whose story is missing and who is needed to create an effective, actionable plan.

Also, think beyond those who agree with you. Think about those who may block your outcomes, as well as those who may have misaligned incentives for wanting to be part of the coalition. These folks may be considered atypical, but by bringing them into the fold, you can hear and see adverse reactions to your efforts from the beginning.

As an ABILPOC leader, you will want to tap into your own experiences. Who was an advocate for you? Who do you wish was telling your story at the decision-making table? At the same time, you also want to think of the identities you don't personally possess and ensure they are also represented in your coalition. In *Building Equity: Policies and Practices to Empower All Learners,* authors Dominique Smith, Nancy Frey, Ian Pumpian, and Douglas Fisher (2017) present an "identity wheel" that includes many characteristics a person may have. You can use it as part of a reflection exercise to see if multiple perspectives are represented in your coalition.

In a small school district in Wisconsin, the message has been that staff are expected to engage with the community as much as possible, in various ways, from attending events to participating in training together. Laurice, the district's equity officer, says the district has been intentional in demystifying structural components such as the special education referral process and the discipline code. She explained:

> Our district equity leadership team is a third community leaders, so we have our advocacy groups, the police department, Boys & Girls Club, Big Brothers Big Sisters, and YMCA. Then we also have a third parents and then a third district administrators and our superintendent.

The Student Equity Leadership Team (SELT) has a different structure and purpose. Here is how Laurice described it:

> Anyone can be part of a SELT team that we now have in middle schools and our high school team. Our Student Equity Leadership Teams also are mirroring a lot of what adults are doing. So things that we are addressing as far as concerns, student experience, perspective, it's all about perspective taking. And now where we're shifting our SELT teams is to be a more formalized advocacy [group] in all the things that we're doing. So new policies. One of the things that was brought up last year was the dress code.

Kori, a Black equity officer in a medium-size charter network in Washington, D.C., said that as soon as she took on her role, her focus was to work in the margins:

> I spent a considerable amount of time talking to people who felt like they weren't in power. Talking to the people who felt like, you know, "I've been here for five years; nobody's ever listened to what I have to say." And so what that ended up doing, in a really beautiful way, I'll be

honest, was having people rally behind something and feel like they were a part of something almost that like the establishment didn't realize.

This approach helped Kori establish credibility and her leadership stance. She explained:

Neutrality is not my friend, and so it's a part of my leadership style to always be clear about where I stand . . . I knew that my strategy was not to be a mouthpiece for the CEO, but rather to be representative of creating a space where the people who were in the margins in the organization had a voice.

Building a diverse network requires building capacity. First getting a sense of the strengths that everyone brings to the table enables you to match, pair, and group folks who will complement and support one another's development. I recognize that I work based on who is in front of me and their needs. I'm OK with slowing down and embracing the messiness of a situation. This reality doesn't dismiss the need for work plans and timeframes. It just means that I need to be paired with someone whose strengths include planning skills. I provide my teammate the opportunity to stay present, and my teammate holds me accountable to keep progressing to meet deadlines.

Manage Political Landmines

As noted earlier, in 2021 state lawmakers began introducing laws to stop school districts from teaching critical race theory. Critical race theory is a theoretical legal framework that provides six tenets for understanding the role of race in the United States. However, the concept has been distorted. According to *Education Week*, as of 2022, 36 states had introduced bills or resolutions to restrict what districts and teachers can teach to students, and 14 states, mainly in the South, had passed these measures. The bills are similar in their goal of eliminating from the school curriculum any topics that explain the true history of the United States, as well as topics focused on the LGBTQIA+ community (Pendharkar, 2022).

These laws have made leaders of color a target. In a 2022 publication titled *The Conflict Campaign: Exploring Local Experiences of the*

Campaign to Ban "Critical Race Theory" in Public K–12 Education in the U.S., 2020–2021 (Pollock et al., 2022), UCLA researchers spoke to 21 equity officers to understand the impact of these new laws on their jobs. In summarizing their interviews with equity officers, the researchers state:

> EOs spoke of "witch hunts" and "increased stress levels" due to "the demands" of anti "CRT" campaigners. Equity officers described campaign tactics such as FOIAing emails, surveilling teaching and professional development through "screenshots," and school board pressure as efforts to censor and control learning experiences to align with the "values" only of critics. Some EOs and other district-level educators responding to our survey shared how a context of threat and "intimidation" led to fear to persist in efforts with both students and teachers. As one EO put it, "Generally, it has led to an overall fear of educators to 'do the work' of DEI because of the vocal minority in our community." (Pollock et al., 2022, p. 8)

This account describes the current climate. Given the history, it will not get better anytime soon. In building your coalition, you will have to be mindful of the politics associated with bringing people together. Every community has formal and informal influencers and authority figures—you need to know them both. Power and privilege have a tight hold in U.S. school systems, so they need to be recognized in coalition building.

As you are carefully building your coalition, you need to be on the lookout for coalitions that may be built against you. These can come in the form of parents, community businesses, and even colleagues. Your work involves asking those who have privilege to give up some of their privilege. To manage these potential landmines, you can use the strategy of having the "meeting before the meeting." Conversations may occur during a formal meeting, or they can occur via a text you send explaining what you need a coalition member to say or do to be a support.

As you move forward with your coalition, it is important and even advisable to support and join others' coalitions. There are always community groups that are working to create change. Taking the time to attend meetings, offer support, and connect with leaders will be critical to keeping your own coalition going.

The community will expect you, as an ABILPOC leader, to be visible and present for the implementation of initiatives—often because system-level leaders dedicated to equity are hired in response to an event or series of events that have led a system to directly address an inequity. Your hiring may also be a result of a community push to diversify leadership. Given these circumstances, you will be seen as a bridge into a dominant culture that has had a negative impact on the community for generations. You will need to be the bridge while managing expectations related to eliminating all the generational trauma.

The work involved in this effort requires time and patience. Recall the example in Chapter 5 of Monica, the equity officer in Florida, who told of meeting with more than 100 people via Zoom, which led to a series of other connections, all of which required good listening skills and the ability to convey understanding and a determination to "make things right."

Tauheedah in Georgia compared her experience with the coalition built by Black Panther Fred Hampton in Chicago in the 1960s: "It reminds me of the Black Panthers meeting with the Neo Nazis and like how people are like, 'How did this even happen?'" She noted the value of looking beyond the "façade of the rhetoric" to see "the humanity of folks."

Add Layers

An effective coalition works in multiple layers of the system. You must engage students as well as system-level leaders. Departments of curriculum and instruction are just as integral as personnel and finance. Many school systems work in silos. Leaders of each division may meet regularly, but they often work on separate islands. To effectively create change, you may have to connect with each division, one at a time, to build each layer of support. This methodical approach to building your coalition will take time but can strengthen your outcome.

Angela in Texas, featured in the vignette that opened this chapter, found the "everyday people" for her internal coalition in school buildings. She started with new teachers and new principals by connecting with them during their induction classes. When her district became part of the Anti-Defamation League's "No Place for Hate" campaign, she was able to interact with people on all of the campuses.

Angela continued to build her internal coalition when she launched a two-year cultural proficiency professional learning experience for staff. The first year focused on staff members learning about and beginning their personal cultural proficiency journey (year 1) and then building their capacity to develop and deliver professional learning (year 2).

This exposure motivated staff members across the district to connect with Angela. They became believers in the impact of teaching and leading with cultural proficiency and worked to make sure she had the support she needed by doing the work at their schools and sharing their experiences with board members.

Angela's internal coalition created stepping-stones to build an external coalition. She began inviting community members to her training for staff to build collective language. This invitation opened the closed doors of the district to a variety of community-based organizations that previously had interacted with the district through formal meetings or even lawsuits as they were pushing for changes within the district. Angela created a learning space for staff and community to come together around the single objective of being better adults for the students they all were serving.

As an ABILPOC leader leading change, your role is to connect the islands. You will be labeled as someone who is looking to change what is comfortable and normal, an effort that will not be universally welcomed. You may experience pushback from other ABILPOC leaders who want to maintain control of the island that they have established for themselves. You may also experience white fragility from white colleagues who are not interested in doing their job differently or more inclusively. These possibilities are why the layered approach is critical. For example, it may take a couple of years to tackle the division leading special education efforts, but the curriculum and instruction division may be ready right away.

Create More Than One Coalition

Developing a community-focused coalition is critical for creating equitable school systems. It is equally critical to have coalitions that will serve you personally and professionally. In other words, as mentioned earlier, you need more than one coalition. You will want a space where you can be free to share and seek advice.

As an ABILPOC leader, you must protect your body, mind, and spirit, and it is reasonable to have a coalition for each of those. Your everyday life is naturally personal, and it can be retraumatizing if you experienced some of the same inequities as a student that you are trying to combat as a leader. In addition, the microaggressions you experience at work will also happen when you are in the grocery store and walking down the block. Coalitions can be a part of self-care.

In a small district in Massachusetts, Jessica, the director for equity and excellence, created an external coalition. When she took the position in 2018, she knew similar roles were being created in other communities. Because her role was new in her district and the job had so many aspects, she felt it would be critical to connect with others. One of her peers had spoken a lot about the value of her job-alike peer group, so Jessica decided to create her own. After doing a Google search for people holding similar positions in other districts throughout Massachusetts, she sent them emails, and they responded.

When they gathered a few months later, everyone brought food and sat down to eat. "I thought it was going to be a structured conversation with an agenda and protocol," Jessica recalls, "but I realized that we all just needed a space to vent with people that understood us because no one else in our districts have our roles."

Everyone in the group is a person of color, but with other intersectional identities. The group now meets virtually or in person every other Friday, and participants welcome the opportunity to say, "This came up in my district. How would you respond?" They share job descriptions and books they are reading, and just vent.

In Maryland, a statewide network of folks who hold equity roles convenes once a month. David, a Black equity officer in a large district, described the benefits:

> I have found within that group, there are spaces of people where I can connect . . . around some authentic conversations and common challenges. I tend to be pretty comfortable naming something and asking the group to process what's happening.

Mariane, the equity officer in California, focused on her student coalition as soon as she assumed the role. She described the experience:

> I really loved being able to kick off and work with the students through the educational and diversity collaborative. . . . And that is a part of the inclusivity, right? Because if we're not including kids at the table when we're talking about their education, we're just not doing it right. Student voice is key to equity in education.

In my case, before I could build external coalitions, I needed a supportive internal coalition. My favorite part of my job description is "put up a mirror to the organization"—but that mirror can become heavy if that work is being done alone. We formed affinity groups for staff members as part of our equity efforts. In the ABILPOC affinity group, I found my coalition. We collectively decided that we wanted the group to have no agenda or formal structure. We wanted it to be a space for healing and affirmation. However, it has also become a space for critical conversations about what we need from the organization and from each other. I soon found myself turning to the affinity group for feedback on staff meetings, for input in developing our DEI goals, and for emotional support.

Now I have built an external coalition. I have pulled together researchers, district leaders, and fellow nonprofit leaders to support the efforts of our organization. This coalition started with individual conversations—being able to share our goals, share my story, and hear their stories and aspirations. I now have relationships with each member of this external coalition, so that I can lean on and learn from them, and they know their support will be reciprocated.

In *Culturally Responsive School Leadership*, author Muhammad Khalifa (2018) describes how "culturally responsive leaders" engage their communities:

> Culturally responsive leaders engage communities in nonexoticizing ways . . . they establish positive rapport and trusting relationships with communities . . . they use community epistemology and elders to craft and revise school policy . . . and perhaps most important, they resist the urge to be neutral or "official" as they enter communities and advocate for community-based goals. (p. 192)

Coalition building is an art, but by following the blueprint of community organizers past and present, you can engage others who will become supporters, thought partners, and cheerleaders inside and outside your school system.

Conclusion

Having started my leadership journey at a young age, I sometimes believed that the purpose of being a leader was to have all the answers. I was quickly proved wrong.

Liberation for ABILPOC leaders and the students and the communities they serve will not come from their leadership alone. Popular perceptions of a single person driving a movement—Gandhi, Martin Luther King Jr., César Chávez—are inaccurate. These prominent figures did not work alone, and neither can you. As the figurehead of a movement, you are responsible for decentering yourself, which is a part of decentering whiteness, and bringing those closest to the margins to the middle.

Key Takeaways

- Coalition builders are collaborative and center those closest to the problem to be solved. You cannot move unless you are in lockstep with those you are serving.
- Internal and external coalitions are necessary for ABILPOC leaders. You will always need to have someone to turn to for support, to be a pulse check, and to keep you moving forward.

- Coalitions need to be focused on a clear goal. This requirement is why so many movements have a clear platform of "asks" they are striving for. A clear goal is also an impetus for bringing people on board.
- Coalitions need diverse participants who represent different silos of a complex system. Coalitions have no separate lanes. Everyone must be willing and able to be in one another's lanes.
- Coalition builders need a political power map. You need to know the formal and informal influencers and authority figures. Power and privilege have a tight hold on our school systems, so they need to be recognized in coalition building.

"Taking It Further" Reflection Questions

- What type of coalitions do I need to build to move past my current situation?
- How can I create coalitions that will fuel my efforts as well as recharge my motivation to keep moving forward?
- What individuals who are doing similar work, within or outside the school system, do I need to connect with?
- What community organizations do I need to connect with to move closer to achieving my goal of creating an equitable school system?
- How am I bridging disparate but similar efforts to create a stronger, more unified effort?

Additional Resources

- IDEO, an international design and consulting firm, has created a collection of articles, tools, and courses to bring its approach to design thinking to many fields, including education.
- The Boston Public Schools' Racial Equity Planning Tool outlines a six-step process intended to ensure that decisions fulfill the goals of closing opportunity gaps and advancing racial equity.
- The Race Equity Cycle Pulse Check, developed by Equity in the Center, offers a way for organizations to check on their progress toward becoming equitable, including next steps and tools to help organizations advance in their efforts.

7

Taking a Stand

If you are neutral in situations of injustice, you have chosen the side of the oppressor.

—Archbishop Desmond Tutu

The phrase Al servicio de usted—*"In service to you"—has been a guide to Jeremy Bogan since he transitioned more than 10 years ago from being a principal to becoming director of language, culture, and equity in a medium-size district in Colorado. He has learned—and unlearned— what it takes to activate others in creating an equitable school system. His wide-ranging duties include, among others, overseeing federal programs, migrant education, community partnerships, and English language development, giving him a sense of how students are doing in more ways than just in the classroom.*

An immigrant from Guatemala, Jeremy personally understands what many of the students in the district are experiencing, but his insight doesn't mean he has not done harm or had to apologize for not making the right decision. As he explains,

I didn't realize how performative I was. And I had to really take a step back and recognize the fact that maybe I haven't been a justice advocate. Maybe I've just thought about it through . . . a focused lens of resource equity. So I had to start really unlearning and learning because I was defensive sometimes. And I had to learn that it's not about not making decisions, it's about making well-informed decisions. And that if I do it correctly, it'll actually be more serving. It'll be better informed. And I will be able to actually elevate marginalized spaces and voices at a higher level.

During this "unlearning," activation with colleagues and community members happened at multiple layers of the system. Here's how Jeremy describes the process:

Over the last 10 years, I've worked really hard at developing an extensive network of people within the community—people from lots of different lived experiences and religious beliefs, great colleagues [from] the Islamic Cultural Center . . . a great leader within our community that started a cultural enrichment center for Black African American youth. So we've been partnering, working with our LGBTQI+ organizations. And then creating an Equity Diversity Advisory Council. I wasn't the first one to start it, but it did stop for a while. And I reactivated it and just personally invited certain people. I did that because I needed their advice, and I needed our leaders to hear their advice.

Jeremy noticed that in addition to people who were activated, there were allies who thought they were ready but were not. He points out the related concern and how to address it:

And they can cause harm as well. So you have to . . . have some assessments and be able to meet with people constantly about their practice—not their beliefs. You don't question beliefs. If they're coming to you, you know they're well-intentioned after you meet with them and through conversation. But how they're going to activate within their practice is just a whole different story. And we see harm being done. We see people *wanting to be culturally responsive and inclusive and developing lessons that are not appropriate.*

Jeremy also took a stand against oppressive policy. He explains what that involved:

Helping people understand that they don't need to defend an institution that is historically oppressive. That the policies that have been developed, we didn't write all of those. Some of them haven't been reviewed since the '90s. Why are we defending that? Let's take a review of it and really decide, Is that serving? Is that relevant to the modern-day district?

A final and foundational activity involved ensuring that the work continues beyond Jeremy's tenure. The district developed a framework called Principles of Community, which include learning about diversity, being inclusive and respectful, and being courageous in actions. The framework also contributed to accountability, and it led to an expanded team including an LGBTQIA+ coordinator, a DEI coordinator, and a restorative practices coordinator. Jeremy explains his rationale:

In order to do it well, a leader needs to concurrently plan an entry plan and a succession plan, because the end goal will not be achieved by one person. And that focus, as well, on policy, so that your actions can be driven by policy, so that the work that is taking place won't ever go away.

Jeremy believes that "you have to push from the bottom up, and I also had to learn that you have to educate at the top and push from the bottom up and then collectively elevate a system."

All Power to the People: Iris Morales as Role Model

Iris Morales grew up in New York City in an era that included the Vietnam War, the assassination of Malcolm X, and the civil rights movement. As the oldest of four daughters of Puerto Rican parents who moved to New York City like many other Puerto Ricans after World War II, she quickly felt the effects of the disparaging inequities her parents dealt with while living and working in a new country (Morales, 2016).

As the primary translator for her mother, Morales saw firsthand the challenges of navigating systems, including speaking to the family's landlord who didn't provide heat or hot water in the winter and the public schools' administrators (Morales, 1980). She refused to let the maltreatment continue. She reached out to a housing organization and rallied other tenants to speak out against the conditions within the apartment building. She later started working with the organization that had inspired the activism that she would continue for decades.

Although her high school guidance counselor didn't provide support, Morales's mother encouraged her to continue her education. Morales applied for and was accepted into a program for "underprivileged students" at the City College of New York, which was seeking to diversify its student population. "At that time, the City University system was only about three percent people of color, with a total of 113 Puerto Rican and Black students in this program," Morales said (Castro, 2021, para. 6). The students created groups that spoke to their lives, interests, and experiences as people of color. In her first year, Morales joined ONYX, the Black organization on campus. She then helped to establish Puerto Ricans Involved in Student Action (PRISA).

In 1968, the groups joined forces to push for increasing admissions of Black and Puerto Rican students, courses in Black and Latine studies, and faculty diversity. Similar efforts were taking place elsewhere in the United States. "The first student uprising took place in Austin, TX, by African American students, and eventually students at other schools such as Brooklyn College and Hunter College were protesting on their campuses," Morales recalled (Castro, 2021, para. 7). Their efforts paid off when City College admissions skyrocketed for Puerto Rican, Black, and poor students in the fall of 1970.

In the spring of 1969, Morales went to the National Youth Chicano Conference in Denver, Colorado, and met members of the Chicago-based Young Lords (also known as the Young Lords Party, or YLP). "Several months after, I found out that the New York chapter was opening an office in East Harlem, so I jumped in and started doing Puerto Rican history classes with people who wanted to join the organization," she said (Castro, 2021, para. 10). She joined the Young Lords in the fall of

1969. The group's early members represented a variety of oppressed people who wanted to see changes in their community. Morales recalled, "There were some Vietnam vets, ex-gang members, lesbians, recovering alcoholics, ex-convicts, Dominicans, Filipinos, Cubans, other Latinx, and 20 percent of the organization, at that time, was African American" (Parra, 2020, para. 14).

In response to community requests, the Young Lords removed the garbage on 110th Street in Harlem, and they got the attention of the city's Sanitation Department by blocking bus routes with the collected trash. They provided free breakfast and clothing in a neighborhood church and conducted door-to-door TB tests, eventually taking over a Tuberculosis Association X-ray van so they could verify results with chest X-rays. They also took over Lincoln Hospital in the Bronx for 12 hours, which led to development of a patient's bill of rights (Morales, 2016). Although the Young Lords remained together for only about seven years, their impact continues.

The Revolution Within the Revolution

The Young Lords modeled themselves after many other social justice groups of the time, including the Black Panther Party and the Brown Berets. All used a military-style structure, which often resulted in women not assuming leadership roles and being relegated to clerical or caretaking duties.

In early 1970, Morales and other women began meeting weekly to discuss issues that mattered to them, forming what was called the Women's Caucus. They read feminist articles and literature and began examining the Young Lords' own publications, including their news-paper, *Pa'lante*, and their 13-point platform. They unpacked terms such as *misogyny, patriarchy,* and *machismo* and reached out to other women activists, including Yuri Kochiyama (whom we met in Chapter 5) and women in the Black Panther Party, the Brown Berets, and other Puerto Rican organizations (Morales, 2016).

The women eventually petitioned the all-male leadership team for changes. Describing the scope of the effort, Morales recalled, "Every-thing had to change . . . the language of how the brothers addressed us had to change. The caucus had to change. The curriculum [of the group's education ministry] had to change. We wanted women's history included. So we had to research it because nobody had taught it to us." Referring to *Pa'lante*, she said, "We wanted women to be writing about what was happening in the world." She noted that "[w]omen initially weren't allowed in the Young Lords' defense ministry, which provided security for the organization as protectors of its members, but also the community." After petitioning for inclusion, women were able to be part of the defense program (Estevez, 2018).

The members of the caucus faced pushback from men in their personal lives as well as men within the Young Lords who thought the focus on women's rights was a distraction within the organization and for the movement as a whole. However, the caucus's efforts resulted in a change in organizational structure, and women were placed in the governing ranks. Morales became the deputy minister of education. The organization also created a Young Men's Caucus whose purpose was to understand internalized racism and women's oppression. Within the organization, male members cooked for children in the free-breakfast program and babysat. Some members resisted the idea of following the directives of a woman, but it became clear that forming a new society meant replacing certain elements of the old one (Morales, 2016).

The caucus's efforts culminated in the "YLP Position Paper on Women," which declared that "Third World Women have an integral role to play in the liberation of all oppressed people as well as in the struggle for the liberation for women." After the paper's release, the leadership team revised the 13-point program and moved equality for women up from Point 10 to Point 5. Point 5 highlighted the desire for equality for women and that in order for that to occur, there could not be any male chauvinism.

A year later, Morales cofounded the Women's Union, which set out to actively recruit women for a mass community movement. The Union was established at the same time the YLP decided to open branches in Puerto Rico. The group developed a 12-point program and put out its own newspaper, *La Luchadora*, written entirely by women (Morales, 2016).

The Women's Caucus and the Women's Union fought against sterilization of Puerto Rican women and for the right to birth control options, including safe abortions. They opened a daycare center in East Harlem, integrated feminist readings into their political education classes, and recruited women of color to social justice activities.

¡Palante, Siempre Palante!

Although the central goal of the YLP was about liberation for Puerto Rico, their membership and efforts were always about all oppressed people, as expressed in the third point of the group's 13-point program and platform. This third point focused on the need for liberation for all oppressed people of the world.

The Young Lords created alliances with women, LGBTQIA+ organizations, and local, state, national, and international struggles. Members of the LGBTQIA+ community participated in all activities and ministries. The opening of a branch on the Lower East Side of Manhattan led to the development of an informal gay caucus. Several Young Lords met with Sylvia Rivera, a Puerto Rican–Venezuelan transgender woman and leader of the Stonewall riots in 1969, and her organization participated in the marches organized by the Young Lords for Puerto Rican Liberation (Morales, 2016).

The women in the Young Lords connected internationally with women activists. In 1971, they attended the Indochinese Women's Conference, where they met with North and South Vietnamese, Cambodian, and Laotian women. In the documentary *Takeover* (Francis-Snyder, 2021), Morales says:

> The Young Lords didn't drop out of the sky one day and all of this happened. We were part of a continuum of history, a legacy that had gone before us. . . . We see ourselves hooking up with Black people, Native Americans, Asians, with other Latinos to form a united front of oppressed people to rage against the real enemy.

Morales left the Young Lords Party in 1974 and went on to attend law school at New York University. In the past few decades, she has continued to serve her community by combining her love of media, historical preservation, and activism to lead nonprofit organizations, write, and produce a documentary (*¡Palante, Siempre Palante!*) on the history of the Young Lords. She also has founded a publishing company, Red Sugarcane Press, an independent agency dedicated to publishing works concerning the Puerto Rican and Latine diasporas in the Americas (Estevez, 2018).

Morales continues to stand for her beliefs and fight for liberation. "You can't have a revolution without two things—racial equality and the equality of women," she says (Estevez, 2018, para. 17).

Competency 8: Be Patient but Persistent

As I've mentioned before, my role as an equity officer didn't come with guidelines or standards; there wasn't even a job description. However, there was an overarching goal to move our organization to become an equitable one. This goal came at the same time as we were experiencing a leadership transition and financial instability. As an organization, we were having good conversations, but the shifts in beliefs and behaviors were slow.

Shifts in policy were even slower. I remember a conversation about our holiday calendar. I was thankful that we were going to stop observing Columbus Day and have a holiday break versus a Christmas break, but I was feeling frustrated when told that my suggestion to change Thanksgiving break to fall break went "too far." Today our internal equity goals are part of our larger strategic plan. We have clear metrics and accountability.

Although my fellow leaders of color have made great strides these past few years, the pendulum has swung back the other way, and the United States is undergoing its latest round of censorship and fragility. As mentioned in Chapter 6, the "conflict campaign" is defined as the purposeful, national/state-interconnected, and locally driven effort to block or restrict proactive teaching and professional development related to race, racism, bias, and many aspects of proactive diversity/equity/inclusion efforts in schools, *while*—for some—gaining political power and control.

In the 2022 study *The Conflict Campaign,* the authors report the following:

> Districts experiencing the most rapid demographic change (in which the percentage of White student enrollment fell by more than 18% since 2000) were more than three times as likely as districts with minimal or no change in the enrollment of White students to be impacted by the localized conflict campaign. (Pollock et al., 2022, p. iv)

As coauthor Mica Pollock notes, "This means that in the very districts where students' families and communities experienced rapid demographic shift, the conflict campaign could particularly restrict students from analyzing that experience—and restrict educators from learning to better support students" (Brown, 2022, para. 18).

These conditions are not only restricting conversations and curriculum, but also adding to the list of reasons why leaders are leaving their positions. The situation amplifies the need to ensure that there isn't just one champion in a school or district, but many.

To be patient but persistent is to know that it will take time to create new liberatory education systems and to acknowledge that the process includes constant trying, evaluating, and retrying—a process that is laborious and slow.

How to Be Patient but Persistent

Among policy and community pushback, being patient but persistent is critical to changing school systems at the institutional level. This involves the following behaviors: giving the "why," avoiding getting trapped, and focusing on policy.

Give the "Why"

Tommy, a Black equity officer in a large district in Georgia, said the "why" needs to be coupled with a strategic timeline: "Everyone wants things *now*. It's not something that is a one-year [effort]; this is the strategic long-term goal that the organization is going to change. It must be strategic." Additionally, Henry, an equity officer in a large district in

Massachusetts, suggested that the strategic "why" needs to be able to tell a story: "How we use data to tell a story is the strategy for the day."

It is not enough to say the "why" only once. You will need to keep saying it, given that the work is a slower undertaking than is suggested by the silver-bullet mentality that we see associated with many education-related initiatives and programming. Saying the "why" is not just something to do in presentations and formal settings. It can come up even in one-on-one conversations to help a colleague slow down, separate their experiences from their students, and hear the story you are trying to tell.

Avoid Getting Trapped

Certain roles come with their own set of assumptions, which can lead to getting stuck in a position that won't lead to change. Stephanie in Texas shared how people can think the role is just about diversity:

> Our team has resisted doing Black history month, Cinco de Mayo, etc. We recognize and celebrate diversity, but it has taken so much work to resist being the office of celebrations, and not to say it's not important, but it's not our role. And I've seen too many equity offices where that becomes a distraction.

Tommy in Georgia learned that he needed to be in on the conversations and meetings where strategic planning and budgeting were happening:

> I think the organization was trying to push me in the space of programming. I had to step back, because they thought I was there to give a book, give a program, give a solution. So my next step was to really start looking at the strategic planning process, getting involved in that, making sure that the voice of equity was there, but not [only] a voice, but a driver. I had to be very strategic about that. So I'd begin to ask questions. "Where in the mission, and vision, and our foundational documents can we find evidence of educational equity and inclusion?"

This effort can be especially difficult if your comfort zone is in celebrations or professional development. I'm not saying that these areas aren't valuable; they are. But you're not going to see systemic change by focusing on them alone. Depending on your leadership role, you may already feel siloed while also bearing a high level of account-ability on your shoulders. To make the work of being an equity officer possible, you will need to control your calendar and where you spend your time. Be your own advocate to ensure that your time is spent in the areas that will have the most impact.

Focus on Policy

A final strategy for being patient yet persistent is to focus on the policy that will last beyond your tenure. When Lisa in Virginia began her career in Maryland, the superintendent encouraged this approach. As she described it, "He came in and was like, 'Nope, we're going to do this work structurally.' We started at the top—school board, leader-ship, having explicit conversations about institutional racism. We ended up developing an equity policy." Tommy in Georgia agreed with this approach: "Get something on paper because the policy is what gives you a backbone. Not just a statement. Put it in policy; put it in the budget; put it in the structure."

Stephanie, the equity officer from Texas, understands that policy may come in the form of practices.

> We do what we call appreciative inquiry. So, if we're looking at pol-icies, we look at what, what do we have that's really strong, that already exists? Let's double down and support that. We have a department that does translation. Let's push to get more than just Spanish translation, but let's look at all of our language popula-tions. And so some of our changes have not been so much policy as they've been practices. I know that our office has made a difference in practices.

In my first year as an equity officer, I used the word *hope* in a conversation with staff. "I hope that we will get to this outcome." I was quickly told that "hope is not a strategy," and the person making that observation was 100 percent correct. I learned that one of the quickest ways to move beyond just hoping is to have a written policy that will provide a course for action.

Competency 9: Take a Stand in Pursuit of a Liberatory Education System Even If It's Unpopular

In 1963, James Baldwin gave a speech titled "A Talk to Teachers." In it, he said this:

> We are living through a very dangerous time. Everyone in this room is in one way or another aware of that. We are in a revolutionary situation, no matter how unpopular that word has become in this country. . . . To any citizen of this country who figures himself as responsible—and particularly those of you who deal with the minds and hearts of young people—you must be prepared to "go for broke." . . . You must understand that in the attempt to correct so many generations of bad faith and cruelty, when it is operating not only in the classroom but in society, you will meet the most fantastic, the most brutal, and the most determined resistance. (Baldwin, 1963b, para. 1)

Baldwin didn't create the term "go for broke." He borrowed it from the 442nd Regimental Combat Team, a group of men who volunteered to fight in World War II while their fellow Japanese Americans were kept against their will in internment camps. Racist policies required the volunteers to be in a separate unit, but it was their unit motto that led them to be one of the most decorated units of service in the history of the U.S. military. A member of this team was Bill, the husband of Yuri Kochiyama, the activist who was featured in Chapter 5.

It's interesting that Baldwin would choose a motto from soldiers to describe what teachers must do, but maybe he was right on target. As bell hooks (1994) wrote, "All of us in the academy and in the culture as a whole are called to renew our minds if we are to transform educational institutions—and society—so that the way we live, teach, and work can reflect our joy in cultural diversity, our passion for justice, and our love of freedom" (p. 34).

Baldwin and hooks are saying that taking a stand and "going for broke" isn't just about teaching and working; it's also about how we live. We should be speaking up in all the spaces we occupy—not just where it's comfortable for us or expected because of the work we do. Ask the difficult questions and take the perspective that will bring about the drastic change necessary to create a liberatory education system.

How to Take a Stand for a Liberatory Education System Even If It's Unpopular

When I unpack the Baldwin quote during a professional learning experience, some leaders feel motivated while others immediately feel overwhelmed. They are not sure they have the capacity to "go for broke" in their current role and circumstance. My response to hesitation is that "going for broke" may change by the day, week, or month and it will look different for every leader, but our students need you to try if we are going to truly change systems. Taking a stand for a liberatory education system even if it's unpopular involves the following behaviors: staying connected to the community, being systematic, always being a teacher, and recognizing that intersectionality matters.

Stay Connected to the Community

"The people closest to the problem are closest to the solution" is a motto held by grassroots organizers and epitomized in what we have learned through leaders from Ella Baker to Iris Morales. Stephanie in Texas has adhered to this motto as well

> When the new superintendent came on board in 2020, I asked if we might have an equity advisory committee, and that gave me a formal way to build a coalition. And so we let our coalitions push because coalitions win. And I always say coalitions win elections, coalitions push policy change. There are a lot of times when I can get beat up and bruised for trying to make recommendations to support policy change, to support students. Because what I'm recommending is disrupting power or questioning power, which is not allowed in hierarchical organizations. And sometimes internal and external community in a collaborative can ask the same questions, sometimes even make demands and challenges to the system.

In Georgia, Tommy learned this first when he was a principal:

I always lead with diversity in mind. That was what I did. And that's how the school transformed into the school they know today, because I took the assets that the students brought to the table instead of looking at it from a deficit mindset and empowered them through who they were through the literature, through the curriculum, and built off their strengths. . . . And we didn't "transform." I say we just "empowered." We just empowered the students that were there and the families.

The importance of staying connected to the community was mentioned by Jeremy in Colorado, as noted at the beginning of the chapter. Centering community is not a stepping-stone to some higher aspiration. Community members have been there before and know what it feels like to be used for personal and professional gain. The community needs to be a central focus as part of the larger effort to ensure an equitable school system.

Be Systematic

Being systematic is not easy. It is not what people are looking for when they want quick solutions or immediate approval. Stephanie in Texas explained:

We meet with departments monthly for two and a half hours, and we do learning experiences. Departments bring their real-world projects to the table, and we apply equity processes and tools. And this keeps people from using us as a check box. . . . It's very challenging for people, but the only way we know how to disrupt the habit and we don't get used as a check box or rubber stamp, because then the organization just keeps doing what it's always done.

Tommy in Georgia said there are three things to focus on if you're going to do systemic change or transformation: systems, the processes that run those systems, and the people. When pursuing systemic change, there are often excuses and roadblocks placed in the way, including no allocated funds and not being part of the formal evaluation system. This led him to ensure the policy was backed up by systems and processes. As he explained:

> I knew I had to get it [equitable practices and policies] from the macro level. So with those systems and attachment to metrics, now it's embedded. It's embedded in what you do. It's not just a good thing to do. It's the right thing to do for the organization and for those that you serve, and it's the fabric of your organization. So it's not just policy, because the policy is a system piece, and even structures are a system piece; but the procedures are essential as well.

In Massachusetts, Harold was part of a four-person team leading the equity office. His role focused on opportunity gaps. The team worked collaboratively to develop a tool that is now used across the district in making decisions. He gave an example of school closures, a topic that can become political and territorial. The tool has given community members the ability to ask questions about the impact of such a decision, such as "Are you closing it down because it's doing bad—because there are about 50 other schools that are also doing bad—so why are we getting closed?" and "Do you just want the land? Because we heard you're going to put retail here."

In my organization, the system we created was a logic model that clearly delineates inputs, activities, and long- and short-term outcomes within a five-year plan. The logic model is shared across the organization and used for accountability; we tie every action tightly to it. The logic model is also fluid, not static. Because it operates within a five-year plan, we step back and adjust at regular intervals.

Each school system may use a different approach for creating and implementing a system, but the underlying commonality is the importance of putting into place guardrails that make it sustainable beyond your leadership.

Always Be a Teacher

Many leaders of color began their career in the classroom. The teaching role is one that should never be forgotten, and it can be leveraged, especially in charged environments. In Georgia, distinguishing between a policy and a resolution has been important. Referring to the controversy over critical race theory, Tommy shared that he needed to educate his community that the Georgia Department of Education had passed something stating their disapproval of critical race theory being taught in schools (a resolution) versus something that had to be integrated into a school district's practices (a policy).

When the anti-CRT movement hit the school systems in the fall of 2020, my first reaction was to teach. I wanted to make sure everyone around me knew what the six tenets of critical race theory are and how it is used in education. The point is, do not shy away from your teaching roots. Maya Angelou told us, "Do the best you can until you know better. Then when you know better, do better" (OWN, 2011). Often our role is to help others learn.

Recognize That Intersectionality Matters

A final strategy for this competency is ensuring that the conversation expands to include all minoritized students and communities. Tommy put it this way:

> I'm not an advocate for one child; I'm an advocate for all children. So I must make sure people know I'm an advocate for all students. No matter your gender, your sexual orientation, your religion, because it's whatever the student brings to the table, they need to feel like they belong and [are] accepted because of who they are.

When I began in my current leadership role, I focused on race. The approach came from the belief and understanding that race is the common denominator in all our statistics. Race is also the most difficult topic for many to talk about. Therefore, if we can talk about race and we can create solutions for racial inequities, we will be able to apply them to other identities. This approach was never intended to ignore the fact of other identities but simply to serve as a starting point. As Iris Morales tells us, the intersection is where liberation happens and where a leader of color must stand in order for true change to happen.

Conclusion

"If everybody likes you, you are doing it wrong." This is a statement that I have embraced. It tells me that I'm pushing in places and spaces that are making people uncomfortable. There's also the 20-60-20 rule of change management created by leadership expert Rod Napier and adapted for social justice by Dolly Chugh. Chugh (2018) says that 20 percent of constituents will be on board and ready to do what's necessary to implement the proposed changes. They're allies and agree with you. Sixty percent will understand the need for change but may be skeptical of it. They may be unaware of the issue or unsure how it fits into their work. They are potential allies if given time for conversation and meaningful interaction. The remaining 20 percent will not be on board at all. They won't hear a word you say, no matter how reasonable, patient, or passionate you are. It is a waste of time and energy to focus on this last 20 percent. To be patient yet persistent and take a stand, you need to decide who you will be spending your time with and how you will spend that time.

Key Takeaways

- Continued self-examination is part of standing up for your beliefs. As you continue your journey to racial consciousness, your insights and beliefs may change. Implement a mechanism to give yourself the time to ensure you are always leading with and through your values.
- There are no single-issue inequities or single identities. Tackling the multiple inequities held by a community can be daunting, but it's necessary to bring about true systemic change.
- There will always be political pushback when working for access and equity for minoritized populations. Different year, same strategy. History tells us that progress will be met with push-back. It's what we do during the pushback that will be telling.
- Shifting policies is more important than shifting beliefs. Our systems and structures were intentionally designed to alienate, suppress, and stamp out minoritized populations. Therefore, liberation can only be achieved though structural change.

"Taking It Further" Reflection Questions

- How have you, in your own identity, perpetuated harm? How are you holding yourself accountable for your own actions?
- What is your personal platform? What are the personal beliefs and outcomes that you are willing to take a stand for?
- Assess your current roles and responsibilities. How can you spend more time in the areas that will ensure the work continues after you leave?
- Assess your strategy for creating an equitable school district. What roles do policies, processes, and people play?
- What is your strategy for managing pushback? How do you know your approach is successful?

Additional Resources

- In the *Educational Leadership* article "Beware of Equity Traps and Tropes," author Jamila Dugan (2021) shares a list of ways a school or district can get in the way of meaningful school equity efforts.
- In *A Data Inquiry Guide for Exploring Equity Issues and Solutions*, MAEC (2021) includes three tools that schools can use to increase equity: (1) an equity audit, (2) a nine-step data inquiry cycle for creating action plans, and (3) school-based case studies describing common equity issues and examples of solutions.
- The Learning Accelerator and Bellwether Education Partners came together to create Real-Time Redesign, a free, open resource that provides leaders with an actionable, inclusive, and rapid process for making targeted improvement toward more equitable and resilient teaching and learning.

8

Creating a New School System

A social movement that only moves people is merely a revolt. A movement that changes both people and institutions is a revolution.

—Martin Luther King Jr., *Why We Can't Wait*

Johnny Cole is director of equity and student supports for the Lexington Public Schools in Lexington, Massachusetts. Describing his job, he says, "I don't really have a lane to drive in. I'm driving in everybody's lane."

As a California-born Indonesian American leading equity work in a suburban school district, Johnny's identity is a part of his work and part of creating a new system. He strives to strike a balance of not allowing himself to be tokenized and used as a puppet, while also spending a lot of time building relationships with people who are going to be able to move mountains with him. "I'm constantly interrogating myself and saying, 'In what ways am I holding true to my values for this work? Am I doing this for the right reasons? Am I perpetuating the inequities by my behaviors, by being complicit with the system? Am I being realistic? Am I being truthful with myself?'" This interrogation threads through Johnny's work with his colleagues, the staff that he supports, and the district community.

The leadership team leans on a quote from author and activist Tim Wise: "Our jobs with young people should be to ratify the experiences, the realities of the people in the margins, and challenge the experiences of those in the center." The quote inspired the personal and professional practice goal for the leadership team. They want to make sure that they are not working just from the white perspective, for example, or from the perspective of the dominant group. Johnny explains that it looks different depending on who we are and what we're doing, whether it's in a school building or elsewhere. The internal questions remain the same: "In what ways am I part of a dominant group that needs to have my experiences challenged to understand that this is not how everyone walks through the world, and in what ways do I need my experiences ratified as a person on the margins, or do I need to do that for my staff or students or families?"

With colleagues and staff, Johnny has held up the mirror for others to continue to build their skills as allies and collaborators. He says a big challenge is convincing white folks that "you're not as far along as you think you are." He describes another challenge as follows:

> *A challenge that I run into with educators of color and students of color is recognizing the ways in which inequity thrives when they engage in oppression Olympics—like "We have it better or worse than that other group." We need to all see how this is impacting us all and fight against it together.*

This tendency to retreat into a group mentality shows up in big and small ways, especially during meetings. Johnny admits that he constantly is negotiating when to speak up and when not to. He explains, "I also rely on some of my white colleagues who I consider allies. I try and hold back and be like, 'Are they going to jump in?' And more often than not, they do, which is fantastic. So that's what I hope will happen more often."

In terms of the community, Johnny is building a lot of trust. He has established relationships with groups in the community that bring together historically marginalized constituency groups, like Indian American, Chinese, and Black residents of the town. They have been valuable partners in making sure that the community is aware of actions that have taken place while also holding the district accountable. They are starting to believe that we are committed to this work.

The district also rolled out identity lessons across all the elementary schools that talked about gender identity in kindergarten. Johnny shared that there was a lesson in the 1st grade that opened the door to discussing police brutality toward African Americans, although it wasn't explicitly for that purpose. When one parent questioned the appropriateness of the lesson, other parents started writing letters to the school committee in support and appreciation of the work.

Transparency is another value Johnny has leaned on in this role— ensuring that community members outside and within the district know what the district is doing and why. He says his efforts rely on key questions:

> How do we get word out to our families of color in our district about how important this is and how we are centering them in this work? How are we authentically honest with our white families about like, "It is true that your students might experience discomfort and marginalization in this work, and that's a good thing for them."

Although Johnny knows and feels the burden of being the one leading the work and being of a minoritized population, he is leaning on colleagues and on his values in every decision and conversation, including those with parents, when, he says, his message is this:

> Our goal is for you to understand what we're doing here, and you as a parent can decide if you want to fight against that in the home. We're doing what we're doing in the schools, and you might even decide to take your child somewhere else to be educated; but this is what we're doing.

Breaking Barriers and Upending Systems:
Pauli Murray as Role Model

Pauli Murray broke barriers, redefined laws, built an interracial community, and inspired others through writing from their days as a young child in North Carolina to their final role as an Episcopal priest. Murray's experiences as a person whose racial appearance and gender expression fell outside Black/white and female/male binaries, coupled with their belief that love is more powerful than hatred, provided a perspective that led them to act in transformational ways (Haney, 1988).

Anna Pauline Murray was born in 1910, the same year that the National Urban League was founded and the year after the NAACP was established. "My life and development paralleled the existence of the two major continuous civil rights organizations in the United States" (Murray, 1987, p. 3).

When Murray was 3, their mother died and they were separated from their siblings and raised by Aunt Pauline. However, Aunt Pauline provided a rootedness that would support Murray in her childhood. Aunt Pauline instilled racial pride, but it couldn't shield Murray from how race and gender showed up in life (Murray, 1987). Murray saw how members of their family "passed" as white for work opportunities or access into stores. They cringed when the white school superintendent said, "You're a credit to your race" when visiting. Murray avoided the segregated streetcars, stores, and theaters as much as possible as a "private protest."

Murray often got in trouble for their energy and unwillingness to follow gender norms in their dress and activities. They favored boy's clothes. Aunt Pauline accepted their enjoyment of physical activities and affectionally called them "my little boy-girl" (Murray, 1987). At 15, they adopted the nickname "Paul." Later they tried out others, including "Pete" and "Dude," then began using "Pauli" while at college and never referred to themself as "Anna" again (Rosenberg, 2017).

After graduating from high school, they chose not to attend a nearby all-Black college and instead moved to New York City and attended an additional year of high school there, to establish residency and secure enrollment into Hunter College, where they orchestrated the beginnings of a Black Student Union in conjunction with the international students (Murray, 1987). In 1938, Murray sent a letter to President and First Lady Roosevelt, expressing disappointment in their silence on racial segregation. Their correspondence with First Lady Roosevelt continued for many years.

Wanting to be closer to their aging aunt, Murray applied for graduate school at the University of North Carolina but, in accordance with the university's policy at the time, was rejected on the basis of race. Murray's attempt to enroll became public knowledge, and they became a symbol of a push for integration. However, the NAACP declined their request for a suit against the university, in part because of concerns about Murray being an out-of-state resident at the time (Murray, 1987).

Murray continued to engage in protest. They were arrested in Virginia for refusing to give up their seat on a bus, and they protested the murder conviction of sharecropper Odell Waller, who was accused of killing his white landlord and executed in 1942. As a law student at Howard University in the 1940s, Murray helped initiate sit-ins at Washington, D.C., restaurants.

At Howard Law School, race was no longer a factor Murray had to deal with in most of their everyday interactions, but gender became central. Murray was the only woman in their law class and often was alienated or silenced by classmates and professors. However, in 1944, in the last year in law school, they wrote a paper challenging the "separate but equal" formula, arguing that segregation violated the Thirteenth and Fourteenth Amendments. Murray asserted that it was time to focus on the constitutionality of segregation. "In essence I was challenging the traditional NAACP tactic of concentrating on the equal side of the Plessy equation" (Murray 1987, p. 298). After receiving an extension on the final paper, "Should the Civil Rights Cases and Plessy v. Ferguson Be Overruled?" Murray spent spring and summer trying to answer this question. They discovered later that it was used by the NAACP lawyers preparing their arguments for Brown v. Board of Education (Murray, 1987).

After graduating from Howard as valedictorian, Murray was rejected from Harvard Law School on account of their sex. In response to this latest exclusion, Murray wrote, "Gentlemen, I would gladly change my sex to meet your requirements, but since the way to such change has not been revealed to me, I have no recourse but to appeal to you to change your minds. Are you to tell me that one is as difficult as the other?" (Mayeri, 2013, p. 87).

Faced with gender challenges, limited employment options, and then isolated work environments, Murray was again propelled to action and activism. In 1965, they coauthored a law review article that argued that Jim Crow, a system of binary racial categorization, had a companion: "Jane Crow." Jane Crow "similarly classified humans into two binary gender categories, segregated the groups and violently policed their intimate interactions, and restricted the economic and political possibilities of those labeled 'woman'" (Fisher, 2016, p. 95). Murray's activism also included being a founding member of the National Organization for Women (NOW). In 1977, they became the first Black woman ordained as an Episcopal priest.

Murray's activism within and outside institutions was happening at the same time they were grappling with their own gender and sexuality. They repeatedly sought out hormone therapy. In personal diaries, they expressed themselves as "one of nature's experiments; a girl who should have been a boy." They didn't like to characterize themself as a lesbian; instead, they considered their "very natural falling in love with the female sex" a result of being male (Rosenberg, 2017).

From a young age until death, Pauli Murray worked to change the situation for themselves and for all of us. Individually and collectively, they pushed against policies and systems that were hindering progress. They never shied away from institutional or personal obstacles that may have seemed intimidating to others. The last words of their final memoir encapsulate their life's work: "There is no north or south, no black or white, no male or female—only the spirit of love and reconciliation drawing us all toward the goal of human wholeness" (Murray, 1987, p. 569).

Competency 10: Act to Change Systemic Racism Every Day in Policies, Procedures, and Systems

The Fourteenth Amendment to the U.S. Constitution, ratified in 1868, was one of three amendments passed during the Reconstruction era to abolish slavery and establish civil and legal rights for Black Americans. It granted citizenship to all persons born or naturalized in the United States and guaranteed all citizens "equal protection of the laws."

The amendment would later become the basis for many landmark Supreme Court decisions over the years, including those regarding segregated schooling (1954's Brown v. Board of Education), the use of contraception (1965's Griswold v. Connecticut), interracial marriage (1967's Loving v. Virginia), abortion rights (1973's Roe v. Wade), and same-sex marriage (2015's Obergefell v. Hodges) (NCC Staff, 2020).

This final competency is asking us to push—every day—to change our education system beyond the level of mindsets and bias, to the level where systems are dismantled and updated to meet the needs of its current students. Pauli Murray showed us what this looks like as life's work. The Fourteenth Amendment shows how a constitutional principle can be used and reused to propel us forward toward a liberated country. How does this level of change show up in our everyday actions?

Although this competency needs to be practiced every day, the desired outcome takes a long time to achieve. In her essay "Revolution: It's Not Neat or Pretty or Quick," poet and activist Pat Parker (1981) alerts us to how challenging liberation is: "The reality is that revolution is not a one-step process: you fight, you win, it's over. It takes years" (p. 240). Parker's words echo those of Audre Lorde (2007), who said, "Revolution is not a one-time event. It is becoming always vigilant for the smallest opportunity to make a genuine change in established, outgrown responses; for instance, it is learning to address each other's difference with respect" (pp. 140–141).

Parker (1981) also emphasizes the need for an intercultural and intersectional approach to practicing this competency:

> Another illusion that we suffer under in this country is that a facet of the population can make revolution. Black people alone cannot make a

revolution in this country. Native American people alone cannot make revolution in this country. Chicanos alone cannot make revolution in this country. Asians alone cannot make revolution in this country. White people alone cannot make revolution in this country. Women alone cannot make revolution in this country. Gay people alone cannot make revolution in this country. And anyone who tries it will not be successful. (p. 241)

As you practice this competency, you will experience a range of emotions. Lorde (2007) warns us how "infinitely complex any move for liberation must be. For we must move against not only those forces which dehumanize us from the outside, but also against those oppressive values which we have been forced to take into ourselves" (p. 135). This disequilibrium requires you to take stock of your emotions and actions—an effort that may be freeing for some and terrifying for others. This state of disequilibrium brings the danger that you could become your own obstacle. Freire (1970) warns of how quickly the oppressed can become the oppressor.

How to Act to Change Systemic Racism Every Day in Policies, Procedures, and Systems

Pauli Murray consistently looked to change at the policy level. Almost all of the leaders I spoke to have similar aspirations. They recognize how school systems are constantly looking to make small changes and shifts that won't cause too much distraction or discomfort, particularly for the adults in the system, but that leads to the same outcomes for students. Acting to change systemic racism in policies, procedures, and systems every day involves the following behaviors: centering students and families, fighting systems with systems, and staying true to your values.

Center Students and Families

The COVID-19 pandemic required leaders to do things differently. As parents and families became primary educators, leaders needed to find new ways to work. If students and their families weren't the center of how a school was run before, there was no other choice but to make them the center if schools wanted students to remain engaged.

TaraShaun, a Black school principal in Illinois, believes student voice has been essential in her culture-and-community approach to leadership. "I'm very transparent [about] what data is used," she said. "I did surveys with my kids about what kind of school they want and why. And then whenever I made a decision that tied back to that, I [would] let them know [that the decision was] based off the results we got in this survey." And when the pandemic came to her school, TaraShaun's pivot wasn't a drastic move, because the school was already a personalized learning environment where student-centered planning and programming was part of everyday practice.

For Shelly, a Black principal in a medium-size district in Texas, centering students meant providing resources:

> We opened up drive-thru pick-up lines and provided every single student with school supplies for the school year. Many of my students, especially those of color, were without any supplies. They were trying to work from home and had nothing. We made sure they had manipulatives, reading resources, graphic organizers, pencils, crayons, notebooks, anything they would have had access to at school. If parents could not get there to pick up [the supplies], we simply delivered them to their homes. It was a time to take the schoolhouse to the family's house, and we did all we could to ensure they had access to all learning resources possible.

At a district level, centering students and family for Tommy in Georgia means them being part of the curriculum analysis process. A committee of students, teachers, and families came together to develop a decision-making matrix to interrogate current curriculum being used in the district and make suggestions for adjustments.

Fight Systems with Systems

The work of changing a school system is to do just that—change the *system*. It is not to try to change *people* to fit into a system that was never designed for them. At the same time, however, Stephanie in Texas warned that it's not enough to disrupt and tear down everything.

There needs to be intentionality in replacing the existing system with something new.

Marco, the Latino principal of a small charter school in California, leveraged a change-management approach to focus on dismantling old systems and replacing them with ones that are sustainable and will outlast his tenure in the role. His school has implemented trauma-informed practice and culturally responsive teaching, and has reimagined family engagement to counter the systems that were doing harm to his students and community.

For David, an equity officer in a large district in Maryland, the systems change centered on the district's leadership pipeline. For two years he worked with different groups, including teachers with international backgrounds; talked about equity and cultural responsiveness; and had people share their stories. All those things signaled to potential leaders, "You, too, belong." This groundwork resulted in the district having a more diverse cohort of people in their aspiring leaders program than ever before.

Hierarchy was the system component that TaraShaun wanted to dismantle as a principal in Illinois. She explained:

> I do not subscribe to hierarchical leadership. I model that we all are a part of the success of the school and that we are an all-hands-on-deck space. I pick up trash if I see it; I fill in for teachers; I work the security desk; I serve and have made lunches due to [staff] shortages. Additionally, [I believe in] creating space for students and staff to enjoy school and be excited about their own success. The community approach to school leadership helped me have everyone be more reflective of their practices, biases, and barriers to success.

Stay True to Your Values

I have participated in and facilitated trainings that include an exercise on values. Working from a long list of suggested values, participants choose those that are most important to them and write each one on a sticky note. Then the facilitator asks the participants to narrow their choices down more and more until only two or three remain. Sometimes, to make the exercise more dramatic, the set-aside sticky notes are tossed into the trash to signify that they are of no use anymore. I have done this exercise many times, and every time, I end up with the same two values: family and trust. These are integral to my everyday life and how I lead.

Marco in California has grounded his leadership in the values of love and courage. He explained his rationale for taking this approach:

> I continue to push myself to live by my values . . . if you live by your values, you can't go wrong with yourself. Like maybe you're doing wrong things, but at least you [can] live with yourself, and you know [what you have done] is the right thing. And so, when I live by my values, regardless of what happens, I'm happy with myself. And maybe there's upset parents or maybe upset staff members, and . . . [that's] cool. I know I did the right thing.

Staying true to his values and trusting himself more has also freed Marco's leadership team. "They feel like you trust them," he said, "and that enables them to own their work more, to make more mistakes, to come up with more solutions, to create a more efficient workflow."

TaraShaun, the principal from Illinois, leans on her values of trust, transparency, and high expectations to lead her school community. "Making everybody a part of the process has really led to success for me." She explained that during the pandemic she saw teachers lower their expectations so much that students were not learning, so she challenged her community to raise the bar while still giving space for grace.

Conclusion

"There is no such thing as a nonracist or race-neutral policy. Every policy in every institution in every community in every nation is producing or sustaining either racial inequity or equity between racial groups." These are the words of Ibram X. Kendi in *How to Be an Antiracist* (2019, p. 18). They can ground ABILPOC leaders in terms of where they are leading within and what they need to lead to. This, along with the need to stay true to your values, is a path to liberation.

Key Takeaways

- Liberation requires policy changes. The United States was built on systems of discrimination, and liberation will happen only when those systems are dismantled and rebuilt.
- You will not achieve liberation by fighting for just one community or one area of oppression. Intersectionality is paramount. Social movements are often tied together by a single issue or point of identity. This strategy has generated progress, but we need to try something different to experience liberation.
- It is easy to oppress when the goal is to liberate unless you are intentional and reflective in every move you make. As a leader, you need to be careful that you are not using your power to oppress.

"Taking It Further" Reflection Questions

- Write your own theory of liberation. What do you think you need to do on an everyday basis to act through a lens of liberation?
- How do your values ground your everyday actions? How do you respond to requests that do not align with your values?
- What are the changes in policy that you would want to see in your school system to create liberation for yourself and the community you serve? What would it take to make those changes?

Additional Resources

- In *Freedom Is a Constant Struggle: Ferguson, Palestine, and the Foundations of a Movement*, Angela Y. Davis (2016) discusses the impacts of previous liberation struggles, from the Black Freedom movement to the South African anti-apartheid movement, and then challenges us to imagine and build a movement for human liberation.
- In *How to Be an Antiracist*, Ibram X. Kendi (2019) shares his personal story about becoming an antiracist to compel readers to go on their own journey. He also interweaves history, law, and

science to show the need to focus on changing policies as a primary lever to form a just and equitable society.

- In *The Quaking of America: An Embodied Guide to Navigating Our Nation's Upheaval and Racial Reckoning*, Resmaa Menakem (2022) provides new body awareness exercises to support readers who have experienced the impact of racialized trauma in the United States after 2016.

Final Thoughts

I fear I may have integrated my people into a burning house.
—Martin Luther King Jr., *Why We Can't Wait*

I want to go back to one of my last interviews. In conversation with a principal, he shared that it was disorienting to see Black women in district-level leadership positions uphold and maintain the institutionally racist school system. In his final reflection, he wondered if ABILPOC leaders who are intimately in touch with their personal selves could continue to be leaders in a systemically racist public school system.

I shouldn't be surprised that many of the leaders I interviewed for this book are no longer in their positions. Many have left the school system and are working as consultants or in nonprofit organizations. Like many others who are part of the "great resignation" of 2020–2021, the dissonance pushed them out. To practice self-care, to not sludge through the mud, these leaders have opted out and into another role.

Initially I felt disheartened by this retreat; it felt like failure. However, maybe not. Maybe it felt more like leaders stepping out of the way; leaders believing they had taken their school system as far as they could; leaders believing that they had built the coalition and capacity to the extent that the work would continue and knowing that the work isn't about them as individuals. The movement continues.

Acknowledgments

Without my family story, this book would not have been possible. I became a teacher because of my personal experiences in school. I became a principal when I connected my story with the story of my mother. I became a systems leader when my daughter's school experience was still the same generations later. I wake up every day wanting to change the story.

I always remember that I am a Rice and there's pride and responsibility in holding that name. I am forever grateful for my family. My best friend and sister Arva who read every page of every draft. My husband Marki who cheered me on at each step. My mom and brother Rondie for being a call away for anything I needed. Zora and Julius—nothing makes me happier than having the privilege of being your mom.

Thank you to Dr. John Jenkins for being my mentor from the beginning of my leadership journey and continued guidance and support. And to Dr. Tanya Manning Yarde for showing me that writing a book is possible. Thank you to Nancy Gutierrez and The Leadership Academy team for all your support through this process.

To all the equity officers and principals that entrusted me to share your truth, thank you.

Thank you to Susan Hills, Liz Wegner, and the rest of the ASCD team who worked to bring all of the pieces of the book together and in the right place.

References

Adams, M., Bell, L. A., & Griffin, P. (Eds.). (1997). *Teaching for diversity and social justice*. Routledge.

Aguilar, E. (2016). *The art of coaching teams: Building resilient communities that transform schools*. Jossey-Bass.

Anderson, C. (2016). *White rage: The unspoken truth of our racial divide*. Bloomsbury.

Anderson, E. (2015). The white space. *Sociology of Race and Ethnicity, 1*(1), 10–21.

Apfelbaum, E. P., Pauker, K., Ambady, N., Sommers, S. R., & Norton, M. I. (2008, September). Learning (not) to talk about race: When older children underperform in social categorization. *Developmental Psychology, 44*(5), 1513–1518.

Araiza, L. (2013). *To march for others: The Black freedom struggle and the United Farm Workers*. University of Pennsylvania Press.

Araiza, L. (2021, April 3). Fred Hampton was right: We must fight racism with cross-racial solidarity. *TRUTHOUT*. https://truthout.org/articles/fred -hampton-was-right-we-must-fight-racism-with-cross-racial-solidarity/

Baldwin, J. (1963a). *The fire next time*. Dial.

Baldwin, J. (1963b). A talk to teachers. Digital Commons@Georgia Southern. https://digitalcommons.georgiasouthern.edu/esed5234-master/44

Baldwin, J. (1969). Sweet Lorraine. In *To be young, gifted, and black: Lorraine Hansberry in her own words*, adapted by R. Nemiroff & L. Hansberry (pp. xvii–xxi). Vintage Books.

Bartanen, B., & Grissom, J. A. (2019, May). School principal race and the hiring and retention of racially diverse teachers (EdWorkingPaper No.19-59). Annenberg Institute at Brown University. http://edworkingpapers.com/ai19-59

Benitez, M., Jr. (2010). Resituating culture centers within a social justice framework: Is there room for examining whiteness? In L. Patton (Ed.), *Culture centers in higher education: Perspectives on identity, theory, and practice* (pp. 119–134). Stylus.

Bernard, E. (Ed.) (2004). *Some of my best friends: Writings on interracial friendships*. Amistad.

Bjork, L. G., & Kowalski, T. J. (Eds.). (2005). *The contemporary superintendent: Preparation, practice, and development*. Corwin.

Branigin, A. (2022, February 24). These students helped overturn a book ban. Now they're pushing for a more inclusive education. *Washington Post*. https://www.washingtonpost.com/lifestyle/2022/02/24/students-book-ban-york-school-district-pennsylvania-curriculum/

Brown, A. R. (2014, September). The recruitment and retention of African American women as public school superintendents. *Journal of Black Studies, 45*(6), 573–593.

Brown, C. R., & Mazza, G. J. (2005). *Leading diverse communities: A how-to guide for moving from healing into action*. Jossey-Bass.

Brown, M. (2022, February 1). Divide over how to teach race plays out more in school districts with shifting demographics, study finds. *CNN*. https://edition.cnn.com/2022/02/01/us/ucla-uc-san-diego-racism-gender-study-findings/index.html

Bryant-Davis, T. (2007). Healing requires recognition. *The Counseling Psychologist, 35*(1), 135–143.

Carolina Federation. (n.d.) *People's platform.* https://carolinafederation.org/peoples-platform/

Castro, G. (2021, October 1). Meet Iris Morales, former Young Lords leader and Latinx rights activist. *POPSUGAR*. https://www.popsugar.com/latina/how-former-young-lords-leader-iris-morales-got-into-activism-48503003

Cherry, M. (2022). *The case for rage: Why anger is essential to anti-racist struggle*. Oxford University Press.

Chicago Public Schools. (n.d.). Equity CURVE. https://www.cps.edu/sites/equity/equity-framework/equity-in-cps/equity-curve/

Chugh, D. (2018). *The person you mean to be: How good people fight bias*. HarperBusiness.

Combahee River Collective. (1986). *The Combahee River Collective statement: Black Feminist organizing in the seventies and eighties*. Kitchen Table: Women of Color Press.

Cooper, B. C. (2019). *Eloquent rage: A black feminist discovers her superpower*. St. Martin.

Crenshaw, K. (1989). Demarginalizing the intersection of race and sex: A Black feminist critique of antidiscrimination doctrine, feminist theory and antiracist politics. *University of Chicago Legal Forum, 1989*(8). http://chicagounbound.uchicago.edu/uclf/vol1989/iss1/8

Davis, A. Y. (2016). *Freedom is a constant struggle: Ferguson, Palestine, and the foundations of a movement*. Haymarket Books.

Davis, B. W., Gooden, M. A., & Micheaux, D. J. (2015). Color-blind leadership: A critical race theory analysis of the ISLLC and ELCC standards. *Educational Administration Quarterly, 51*(3), 335–371.

DeAngelis, T. (2019, February). The legacy of trauma: An emerging line of research is exploring how historical and cultural traumas affect survivors' children for generations to come. *Monitor on Psychology, 50*(2), 36. https://www.apa.org/monitor/2019/02/legacy-trauma

Dream Defenders. (n.d.). Our story. https://dreamdefenders.org/our-story/

Du Bois, W. E. B. (1897, August). Strivings of the Negro people. *Atlantic Monthly*. https://www.theatlantic.com/magazine/archive/1897/08/strivings-of-the-negro-people/305446/

Dugan, J. (2021, March). Beware of equity traps and tropes. *Educational Leadership, 78*(6). https://www.ascd.org/el/articles/beware-of-equity-traps-and-tropes

Estevez, M. (2018, October 11). The revolutionary Latinx who brought feminism to a 60s leftist group. *Vice*. https://www.vice.com/en/article/yw9eej/iris-morales-feminist-latinx-young-lords

Fairclough, A. (2000, June). Being in the field of education and also being a Negro . . . seems . . . tragic: Black teachers in the Jim Crow South. *Journal of American History, 87*(1), 65–91.

Feger, H. V. (1942, March). A girl who became a great woman. *Negro History Bulletin, 5*(6), 123.

Fisher, S. D. E. (2016, May). Pauli Murray's Peter panic: Perspectives from the margins of gender and race in Jim Crow America. *Transgender Studies Quarterly, 3*(1–2), 95–103.

Francis-Snyder, E. (2021). Takeover: How we occupied a hospital and changed public health care [video]. *NYTimes Op-Docs*. https://www.nytimes.com/2021/10/12/opinion/young-lords-nyc-activism-takeover.html

Freire, P. (1970). *Pedagogy of the oppressed*. Herder & Herder.

Fujino, D. (2009). Grassroots leadership and Afro-Asian solidarities: Yuri Kochiyama's humanizing radicalism. In D. F. Gore, J. Theodaris, & K. Woodard (Eds.), *Want to start a revolution? Radical women in the Black freedom struggle* (pp. 294–316). New York University Press.

Ganz, M. (2000, January). Resources and resourcefulness: Strategic capacity in the unionization of California agriculture, 1959–1966. *American Journal of Sociology, 105*(4), 1003–1062.

Gere, A. R. (2005, Spring). Indian heart/white man's head: Native-American teachers in Indian schools, 1880–1930. *History of Education Quarterly, 45*(1), 38–65.

Godoy, M. (2017, September 17). Dolores Huerta: The civil rights icon who showed farmworkers "Sí se puede." *NPR*. https://www.npr.org/sections/thesalt/2017/09/17/551490281/dolores-huerta-the-civil-rights-icon-who-showed-farmworkers-si-se-puede

González, J. (2000). *Harvest of empire: A history of Latinos in America.* Viking Press.

Greene, J. P., & Paul, J. D. (2021, October 19). Equity elementary: "Diversity, equity, and inclusion" staff in public schools. Center for Education Policy, The Heritage Foundation. https://www.heritage.org/education/report/equity-elementary-diversity-equity-and-inclusion-staff-public-schools

Gutfreund, Z. (2019). *Speaking American: Language education and citizenship in twentieth-century Los Angeles.* University of Oklahoma Press.

Ha, T.-H. (2014, December 15). *The end of racism starts with each of us: Q&A with Verna Myers.* https://ideas.ted.com/little-by-little-we-can-end-the-war-of-racism-inside-ourselves-qa-with-verna-myers/

Hammond, Z. (2015). *Culturally responsive teaching and the brain: Promoting authentic engagement and rigor among culturally and linguistically diverse students.* Corwin.

Haney, E. (1988, Fall). Pauli Murray: Acting and remembering. *Journal of Feminist Studies in Religion, 4*(2), 75–79.

Harris, C. I. (1993, June). Whiteness as property. *Harvard Law Review, 106*(8), 1707–1791. https://harvardlawreview.org/1993/06/whiteness-as-property/

Harro, B. (2000). The cycle of socialization. In M. Adams, W. Blumenfeld, H. Hackman, M. Peters, & X. Zuniga (Eds.), *Readings for diversity and social justice* (pp. 16–21). Routledge.

Hegde, S. (2022, June 8). What is internalized oppression? *Science ABC.* https://www.scienceabc.com/social-science/what-is-internalized-oppression-definition-h3h3-example.html

Hodgkinson, H. L., & Montenegro, X. (1999). The U.S. school superintendent: The invisible CEO [report]. Institute for Educational Leadership.

hooks, b. (1994). *Teaching to transgress: Education as the practice of freedom.* Routledge.

hooks, b. (1995). *Killing rage: Ending racism.* Henry Holt.

hooks, b. (2000). *All about love: New visions.* William Morrow.

hooks, b. (2001). *Salvation: Black people and love.* William Morrow.

Hung, M. (2002, March 13). The last revolutionary. *East Bay Express.* https://eastbayexpress.com/the-last-revolutionary-1/

InterAction. (n.d). *Our history.* InterAction. http://interactioninc.org/

Irby, D., Green, T., Ishimaru, A. M., Clark, S. P., & Han, A. (2021). *K–12 equity directors: Configuring the role for impact.* Center for Urban Education Leadership. https://urbanedleadership.org/wp-content/uploads/2021/03/K12EquityDirectorsConfiguringtheRole.pdf

James, T. (1987, February). The education of Japanese Americans at Tule Lake, 1942–1946. *Pacific Historical Review, 56*(1), 25–58.

Johnson, B. H. (2005). *Revolution in Texas: How a forgotten rebellion and its bloody suppression turned Mexicans into Americans.* Yale University Press.

Jones, C., & Shorter-Gooden, K. (2003). *Shifting: The double lives of Black women in America.* HarperCollins.

Karpinski, C. F. (2006, May). Bearing the burden of desegregation: Black principals and *Brown. Urban Education, 41*(3), 237–276.

Kendi, I. X. (2019). *How to be an antiracist.* One World.

Khalifa, M. A. (2018). *Culturally responsive school leadership.* Harvard Education Press.

King, D. K. (1988, Autumn). Multiple jeopardy, multiple consciousness: The context of a Black feminist ideology. *Signs: Journal of Women in Culture and Society, 14*(1), 42–72.

King, M. L., Jr. (2000). *Why we can't wait.* Penguin.

King, M. L., Jr. (2007). The mastery of fear [Sermon]. In C. Carson, S. Carson, S. Englander, T. Jackson, & G. L. Smith (Eds.), *The papers of Martin Luther King, Jr., Vol. VI: Advocate of the social gospel, September 1948–March 1963.* University of California Press.

Kochiyama, Y. (1994). The impact of Malcolm X on Asian-American politics and activism. In J. Jennings (Ed.), *Blacks, Latinos, and Asians in urban America: Status and prospects for politics and activism* (pp. 129–141). Praeger.

Lawrence-Lightfoot, S. (2016). Commentary: Portraiture methodology: Blending art and science. *Learning Landscapes, 9*(2), 19–27.

Lax, D. A., & Sebenius, J. K. (2006). *3-D negotiation: Powerful tools to change the game in your most important deals.* Harvard Business School Press.

Leadership Academy. (2021). *A portrait of a culturally responsive school.* https://www.leadershipacademy.org/wp-content/uploads/2021/03/Portrait-of-a-Culturally-Responsive-School.pdf

Library of Congress. (n.d.). The murder of Emmett Till. https://www.loc.gov/collections/civil-rights-history-project/articles-and-essays/murder-of-emmett-till/

Lorde, A. (2007). *Sister outsider: Essays and speeches.* Crossing.

Love, B. L. (2019). *We want to do more than survive: Abolitionist teaching and the pursuit of educational freedom.* Beacon.

Love, B., DeJong, K., Hughbanks, C., Kent-Katz, J., & Williams, T. (2008). *Critical liberation theory.* University of Massachusetts Amherst.

Lyon, C. (n.d.). Loyalty questionnaire. *Densho Encyclopedia.* https://encyclopedia.densho.org/Loyalty_questionnaire/

MAEC. (2021, March). *A data inquiry guide for exploring equity issues and solutions.* https://maec.org/data-inquiry

Mahaye, N. (2018, August 5). The philosophy of Ubuntu in education. https://www.linkedin.com/pulse/philosophy-ubuntu-education-ngogi-mahaye/

Mann, H. (1848). Twelfth annual report. In L. Cremin (Ed.), *The republic and the school: Horace Mann on the education of free men* (pp. 79–80, 84–89). Teachers College Press.

Markstrom, C. A., & Iborra, A. (2003). Adolescent identity formation and rites of passage: The Navajo Kinaaldá ceremony for girls. *Journal of Research on Adolescence, 13*(4), 399–425.

Mayeri, S. (2013). Pauli Murray and the twentieth-century quest for legal and social equality. *Indiana Journal of Law and Social Equality, 2*(1), 80–90.

Menakem, R. (2017). *My grandmother's hands: Racialized trauma and the pathway to mending our hearts and bodies.* Central Recovery Press.

Menakem, R. (2022). *The quaking of America: An embodied guide to navigating our nation's upheaval and racial reckoning.* Central Recovery Press.

Michals, D. (2015). Dolores Huerta. National Women's History Museum. https://www.womenshistory.org/education-resources/biographies/dolores-huerta

Miller, J. B. (2008). Connections, disconnections, and violations. *Feminism & Psychology, 18*(3), 368–380.

Mojica Rodríguez, P. D. (2021). *For brown girls with sharp edges and tender hearts: A love letter to women of color.* Seal.

Molinsky, A. (2016, July 29). If you're not outside your comfort zone, you won't learn anything. *Harvard Business Review.* https://hbr.org/2016/07/if-youre-not-outside-your-comfort-zone-you-wont-learn-anything

Moody, C. D. (1973, May). The Black superintendent. *The School Review, 81*(3), 375–382.

Morales, I. (1980). I became the one that translated . . . the go-between. In A. López (Ed.), *The Puerto Ricans: Their history, culture, and society* (pp. 439–446). Schenkman.

Morales, I. (2016). *Through the eyes of rebel women: The Young Lords: 1969–1976.* Red Sugarcane.

Morris, A., & Staggenborg, S. (2004). Leadership in social movements. In D. A. Snow, S. A. Soule, & H. Kreisi (Eds.), *The Blackwell companion to social movements* (pp. 171–196). Blackwell.

Murray, P. (1987). *Song in a weary throat: An American pilgrimage.* Harper & Row.

Murray, P. (2018). *Dark testament and other poems* (paperback ed.). Liveright.

Myers, V. (2014). *How to overcome our biases? Walk boldly toward them* [video]. TEDxBeacon Street. https://www.ted.com/talks/verna_myers_how_to_overcome_our_biases_walk_boldly_toward_them?language=en

National Center for Education Statistics (NCES). (2022a). Characteristics of public school principals. *Condition of Education.* U.S. Department

of Education, Institute of Education Sciences. https://nces.ed.gov
/programs/coe/indicator/cls

National Center for Education Statistics (NCES). (2022b). Racial/ethnic enrollment in public schools. *Condition of Education*. U.S. Department of Education, Institute of Education Sciences. https://nces.ed.gov /programs/coe/indicator/cge.

National Equity Project. (2012). The lens of systemic oppression. https:// www.nationalequityproject.org/frameworks/lens-of-systemic-oppression.

National Policy Board for Educational Administration. (2015). *Professional standards for educational leaders*. http://www.npbea.org/wp-content /uploads/2017/06/Professional-Standards-for-Educational-Leaders _2015.pdf

NCC Staff. (2020, July 9). 10 Supreme Court cases about the 14th Amendment. *Constitution Center*. https://constitutioncenter.org/blog/10-huge -supreme-court-cases-about-the-14th-amendment

Nemiroff, R., & Hansberry, L. (1970). *To be young, gifted, and black: Lorraine Hansberry in her own words.* Vintage Books.

Nepstad, S. E., & Bob, C. (2006). When do leaders matter? Hypotheses on leadership dynamics in social movements. *Mobilization, 11*(1).

Okun, T. (2021, May). White supremacy culture–still here. https://www .whitesupremacyculture.info/

Okun, T., & Jones, K. (2001). White supremacy culture. *Dismantling racism: A workbook for social change groups*. ChangeWork.

Oluo, I. (2018). *So you want to talk about race*. Seal.

Owens, L. R. (2020). *Love and rage: The path of liberation through anger.* North Atlantic Books.

OWN. (2011, October 19). The powerful lesson Maya Angelou taught Oprah [video]. Oprah.com. https://www.oprah.com/oprahs-lifeclass/the -powerful-lesson-maya-angelou-taught-oprah-video

Parker, P. (1981). Revolution: It's not neat or pretty or quick. In C. Moraga & G. Anzaldua (Eds.), *This bridge called my back: Writings by radical women of color* (pp. 238–242). Persephone.

Parker, P. (2018). *The art of gathering: How we meet and why it matters*. Riverhead Books.

Parker, P. (2019). *3 steps to turn everyday get-togethers into transformative gatherings* [video]. TED Conferences. https://www.ted.com/talks/priya _parker_3_steps_to_turn_everyday_get_togethers_into_transformative _gatherings?language=en

Parra, D. (2020, June 24). Former Young Lords reflect on protests, racism and police violence. *City Limits*. https://citylimits.org/2020/06/24/former -young-lords-reflect-on-protests-racism-and-police-violence/

Peabody, E. P. (1886). *Sarah Winnemucca's practical solution to the Indian problem: A letter to Dr. Lyman Abbot of the "Christian Union."* John Wilson and Son.

Peabody, E. P. (1887). *The Piutes: Second report of the model school of Sarah Winnemucca 1886–87.* John Wilson and Son.

Pendharkar, E. (2022, January 27). Efforts to ban critical race theory could restrict teaching for a third of America's kids. *Education Week.* https://www.edweek.org/leadership/efforts-to-ban-critical-race-theory-now-restrict-teaching-for-a-third-of-americas-kids/2022/01

Perry, I. (2018). *Looking for Lorraine: The radiant and radical life of Lorraine Hansberry.* Beacon.

Pollock, M., & Rogers, J., with Kwako, A., Matschiner, A., Kendall, R., Bingener, C., Reece, E., Kennedy, B., & Howard, J. (2022, January). *The conflict campaign: Exploring local experiences of the campaign to ban "critical race theory" in public K–12 education in the U.S., 2020–2021.* UCLA's Institute for Democracy, Education, and Access. https://idea.gseis.ucla.edu/publications/the-conflict-campaign/

Rabow, J. (2014.). Models of identity development. https://www.academia.edu/4256205/Models_of_Racial_Identity

Racial Equity Tools. (2020). Racial equity tools glossary. https://www.racialequitytools.org/glossary/

Ransby, B. (2003). *Ella Baker and the Black freedom movement: A radical democratic vision.* University of North Carolina Press.

Robinson, K., & Muir, T. (Co-hosts). (2021, March). *Running Realized* (Podcast). https://runningforreal.com/running-realized-episode-three-the-inner-disconnect/

Rose, M. (1990). Traditional and nontraditional patterns of female activism in the United Farm Workers of America. *Frontiers: A Journal of Women Studies, 11,* 26–32.

Rosenberg, R. (2017). *Jane Crow: The life of Pauli Murray.* Oxford University Press.

Rosner, H. (2021, October 14). A philosopher's defense of anger. *The New Yorker.* https://www.newyorker.com/culture/q-and-a/a-philosophers-defense-of-anger

San Miguel, G., Jr. (1987). *"Let all of them take heed": Mexican Americans and the campaign for education equality in Texas, 1910–1981.* University of Texas Press.

Scott, H. J. (1980). *The Black school superintendent: Messiah or scapegoat?* Howard University Press.

Sealey-Ruiz, Y. (2021). *The peace chronicles.* Kaleidoscope Vibrations.

Singleton, G. E. (2005). *Courageous conversations about race: A field guide for achieving equity in schools.* Corwin.

Smith, D., Frey, N., Pumpian, I., & Fisher, D. (2017). *Building equity: Policies and practices to empower all learners.* ASCD.

Spraggins, T. (1970). *Historical highlights in the education of Black Americans.* Center for Human Relations, National Education Association.

Steele, C. M. (2010). *Whistling Vivaldi: How stereotypes affect us and what we can do.* W. W. Norton.

Sue, D. W. (2015). *Race talk and the conspiracy of silence: Understanding and facilitating difficult dialogues on race.* Wiley.

Suyemoto, K. L., & Kim, G. S. (2005). Journeys through diverse terrains: Multiple identities and social contexts in individual therapy. In M. Pravder Mirkin, K. L. Suyemoto, & B. F. Okun (Eds.), *Psychotherapy with women: Exploring diverse contexts and identities* (pp. 9–41). Guilford.

Taie, S., & Goldring, R. (2020, September). *Characteristics of public and private elementary and secondary school teachers in the United States: Results from the 2017–18 National Teacher and Principal Survey first look* (NCES 2020-142). National Center for Education Statistics, U.S. Department of Education. https://nces.ed.gov/pubsearch/pubsinfo.asp?pubid=2020142

Tatum, B. D. (1997). *Why are all the black kids sitting together in the cafeteria? And other conversations about race.* Basic Books.

Tatum, B. D. (2008). *Can we talk about race? And other conversations in an era of school resegregation.* Beacon.

Thom, K. C. (2019). *I hope we choose love: A trans girl's notes from the end of the world.* Arsenal Pulp Press.

Tienken, C. H. (Ed.). (2021). *The American superintendent 2020 decennial study.* Rowman & Littlefield.

Tillman, L. C. (2002). Culturally sensitive research approaches: An African-American perspective. *Educational Researcher, 31*(9), 3–12.

Timm, J. C. (2021, November 25). Georgia teens become unlikely warriors in redistricting fight. *NBC News.* https://www.nbcnews.com/politics/elections/georgia-teens-become-unlikely-warriors-redistricting-fight-n1284351

Tippett, K. (Host). (2016, May). Olympians are chosen by the gods. *On being with Krista Tippett* (Podcast). https://onbeing.org/programs/olympians-chosen-gods-billy-mills/

Tutu, D. (1999). *No future without forgiveness.* Doubleday.

Tyack, D. B. (1976). Pilgrim's progress: Toward a social history of the school superintendency, 1860–1960. *History of Education Quarterly, 16*(3), 257–300.

U.S. Constitution. (n.d.). Amendment XIV. National Constitution Center. https://constitutioncenter.org/interactive-constitution/amendment/amendment-xiv on 04.24.22.

Valverde, L. A., & Brown, F. (1988). Influences on leadership development among racial and ethnic minorities. In N. J. Boyan (Ed.), *Handbook of research on educational administration: A project of the American Educational Research Association* (pp. 143–158). Longman.

Van Dyke, N., & McCammon, H. J. (Eds.). (2010). *Strategic alliances: Coalition building and social movements.* University of Minnesota Press.

West, C. (1994). *Race matters*. Audio Partners.

Wheatley, M. J. (2009). *Turning to one another: Simple conversations to restore hope to the future*. Berrett-Koehler.

Williams, D. A., & Wade-Golden, K. C. (2007). *The chief diversity officer: A primer for college and university presidents*. American Council on Education.

Worthington, R. L., Stanley, C. A., & Smith, D. G. (2020). *Standards of professional practice for chief diversity officers in higher education 2.0.* The National Association of Diversity Officers in Higher Education. https://nadohe.memberclicks.net/assets/2020SPPI/__NADOHE %20SPP2.0_200131_FinalFormatted.pdf

Zambrana, R. E., & Hurtado, S. (Eds.). (2015). *The magic key: The educational journey of Mexican Americans from K–12 to college and beyond*. University of Texas Press.

Zebian, N. (2016). *Finding home through poetry* [video]. TEDxCoventGardenWomen. https://www.youtube.com /watch?v=rNRygxe_8Ys

Zitkala-Sa. (2000). The school days of an Indian girl. In S. H. Smith & M. Dawson (Eds.), *The American 1890s: A cultural reader* (pp. 349–360). Duke University Press.

Index

The letter *f* following a page number denotes a figure.

About the Author

Mary Rice-Boothe, EdD, has more than 25 years of experience in education as a teacher, principal, principal coach, curriculum designer, and equity officer. She currently serves as an executive director of curriculum development and equity at The Leadership Academy, a national nonprofit organization. In this role, she oversees the organization's internal and external equity strategy. She is also the lead designer for the organization's instructional tools and resources.

Mary began her career in education as a high school English teacher in East Harlem. She is a certified Courageous Conversations About Race Affiliate and a certified Facilitative Leadership Trainer. She sits on the board of Marathon Kids. Mary holds a BA in Metropolitan

Studies from New York University, an MA in English and English Education from the City College of New York, and a doctorate in Leadership and Organizational Change from the University of Southern California. She lives in Round Rock, Texas, with her mom, husband, daughter, and son.

Related ASCD Resources

At the time of publication, the following resources were available (ASCD stock numbers in parentheses).

Building Equity: Policies and Practices to Empower All Learners by Dominique Smith, Nancy Frey, Ian Pumpian, and Douglas Fisher (#117031)

Culture, Class, and Race: Constructive Conversations That Unite and Energize Your School and Community by Brenda CampbellJones, Shannon Keeny, and Franklin CampbellJones (#118010)

Cultural Competence Now: 56 Exercises to Help Educators Understand and Challenge Bias, Racism, and Privilege by Vernita Mayfield (#118043)

Equity in Data: A Framework for What Counts in Schools by Andrew Knips, Sonya Lopez, Michael Savoy, and Kendall LaParo (#122021)

Excellence Through Equity: Five Principles of Courageous Leadership to Guide Achievement for Every Student by Alan M. Blankstein and Pedro Noguera with Lorena Kelly (#116070)

Five Practices for Equity-Focused School Leadership by Sharon I. Radd, Gretchen Givens Generett, Mark Anthony Gooden, and George Theoharis (#120008)

Fix Injustice, Not Kids and Other Principles for Transformative Equity Leadership by Paul Gorski and Katy Swalwell (#120012)

Leading Your School Toward Equity: A Practical Framework for Walking the Talk by Dwayne Chism (#123003)

Support and Retain Educators of Color: 6 Principles for Culturally Affirming Leadership by Andrea Terrero Gabbadon (#123018)

For up-to-date information about ASCD resources, go to **www.ascd.org.** You can search the complete archives of *Educational Leadership* at **www.ascd.org/el.** To contact us, send an email to member@ascd.org or call 1-800-933-2723 or 703-578-9600.

THE WHOLE CHILD

The ASCD Whole Child approach is an effort to transition from a focus on narrowly defined academic achievement to one that promotes the long-term development and success of all children. Through this approach, ASCD supports educators, families, community members, and policymakers as they move from a vision about educating the whole child to sustainable, collaborative actions.

Leading Within Systems of Inequity in Education relates to the **safe** tenet.

For more about the ASCD Whole Child approach, visit **www.ascd.org/wholechild.**

WHOLE CHILD
TENETS

1 HEALTHY
Each student enters school healthy and learns about and practices a healthy lifestyle.

2 SAFE
Each student learns in an environment that is physically and emotionally safe for students and adults.

3 ENGAGED
Each student is actively engaged in learning and is connected to the school and broader community.

4 SUPPORTED
Each student has access to personalized learning and is supported by qualified, caring adults.

5 CHALLENGED
Each student is challenged academically and prepared for success in college or further study and for employment and participation in a global environment.